ROCKWEED-COVERED SEA LEDGE AT PEMAQUID POINT, MAINE

SUNDOWN AT HACKETTS COVE, NOVA SCOTIA

A COLONY OF COMMON MURRES ON FUNK ISLAND, NEWFOUNDLAND

SURF FROM A NOR'EASTER

SPREADING LICHEN AT AN ISLAND'S EDGE

A SUMMER GALE ALONG A SCULPTURED SHORELINE

A HARBOR SEAL SCOUTING THE SURFACE

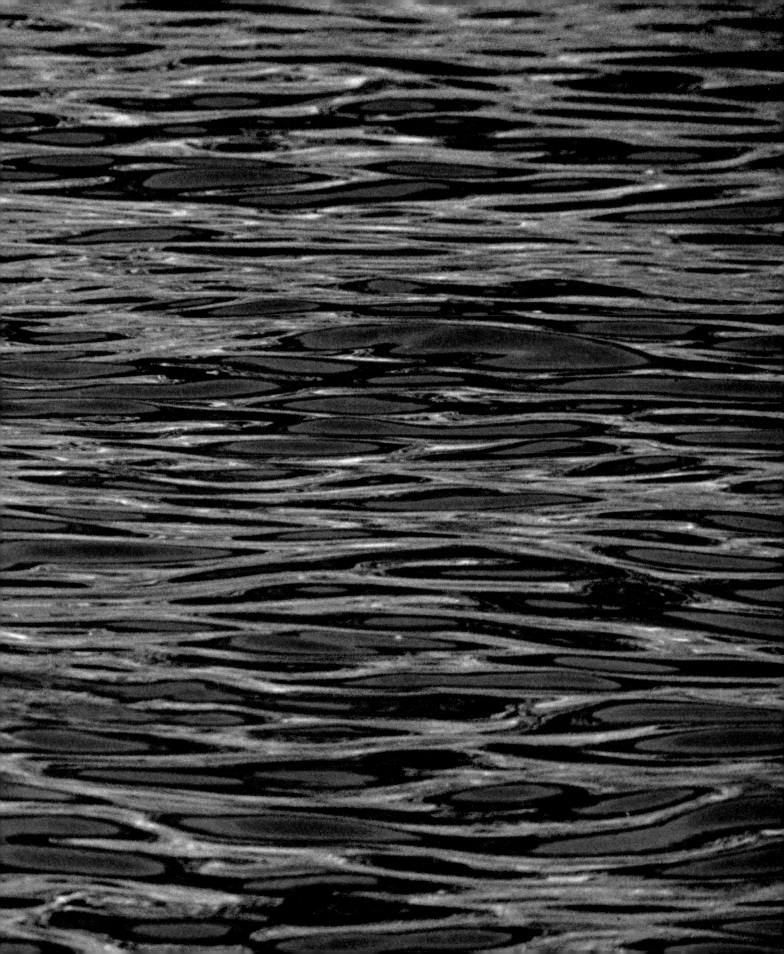

LIFE WORLD LIBRARY
LIFE NATURE LIBRARY
TIME READING PROGRAM
THE LIFE HISTORY OF THE UNITED STATES
LIFE SCIENCE LIBRARY
GREAT AGES OF MAN
TIME-LIFE LIBRARY OF ART
TIME-LIFE LIBRARY OF AMERICA
FOODS OF THE WORLD
THIS FABULOUS CENTURY
LIFE LIBRARY OF PHOTOGRAPHY
THE TIME-LIFE ENCYCLOPEDIA OF GARDENING
FAMILY LIBRARY
  THE TIME-LIFE BOOK OF FAMILY FINANCE
  THE TIME-LIFE FAMILY LEGAL GUIDE
THE AMERICAN WILDERNESS

THE NORTHEAST COAST

THE AMERICAN WILDERNESS/TIME-LIFE BOOKS/NEW YORK

BY MAITLAND A. EDEY
AND THE EDITORS OF TIME-LIFE BOOKS

THE AMERICAN WILDERNESS
SERIES EDITOR: Charles Osborne

Editorial Staff for *The Northeast Coast:*
Text Editor: L. Robert Tschirky
Picture Editor: Mary Y. Steinbauer
Designer: Charles Mikolaycak
Staff Writers: Gerald Simons,
Bryce S. Walker
Chief Researcher: Martha T. Goolrick
Researchers: Joan Chambers,
Helen M. Hinkle, Margo Dryden,
Villette Harris, Mollie E. C. Webster,
Timberlake Wertenbaker
Design Assistant: Mervyn Clay

Editorial Production
Production Editor: Douglas B. Graham
Quality Director: Robert L. Young
Assistant: James J. Cox
Copy Staff: Rosalind Stubenberg,
Eleanore W. Karsten, Florence Keith
Picture Department: Dolores A. Littles,
Joan Lynch

Valuable assistance was given by the
following departments and individuals
of Time Inc.: Editorial Production, Nor-
man Airey, Nicholas Costino Jr.; Library, Peter Draz; Picture Collection,
Doris O'Neil; Photographic Laboratory,
George Karas; TIME-LIFE News Service,
Murray J. Gart.

The Author: For Maitland A. Edey the
Northeast coast blends two lifelong in-
terests: natural history and the sea. He
has sailed small boats all his life, has
cruised often among the Maine islands
and along the shores of New Brunswick, Nova Scotia and Quebec. He also
crossed the Atlantic in 1957 as a working crew member of the *Mayflower II,*
a replica of the original vessel. As a
natural history lover, he conceived and
produced the 25 volumes of the LIFE Nature Library. While he was Editor of
TIME-LIFE BOOKS, he wrote *The Cats of
Africa,* which grew out of four safari
trips taken between 1962 and 1968. He
has also published two books on or-
nithology and a number of articles and
photographs on natural history.

The Cover: Seen from the air, a section
of coastline in southwestern Newfoundland forms a ragged frame around
a bay gleaming with reflected sunlight.
This rocky stretch, identified as a
"drowned," or sea-invaded, coast by its
many inlets, islets and fingerlike prom-
ontories, is typical of the northeastern
shoreline all the way from Newfoundland to southern Maine.

Contents

A Wild Domain Framed by Rock and Sea

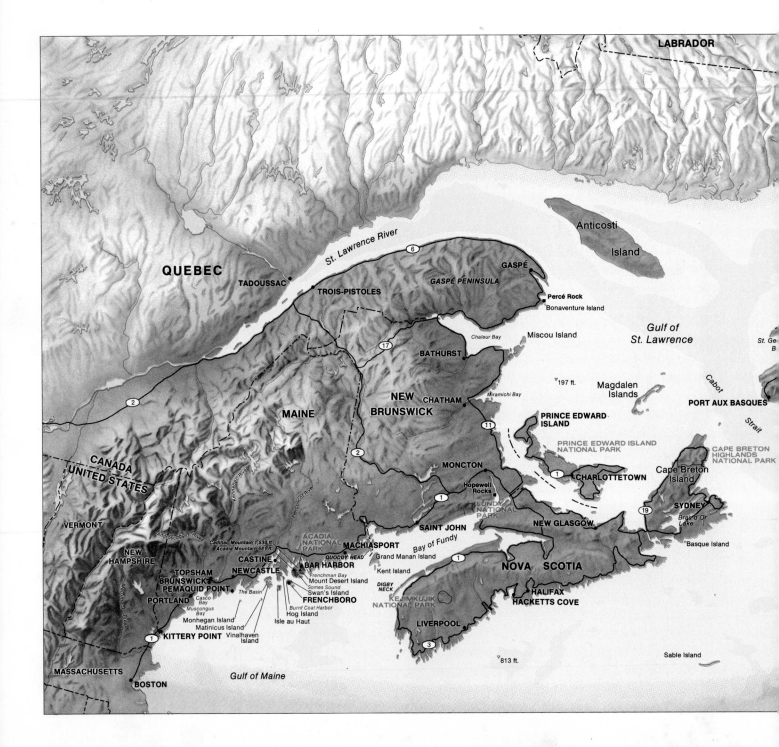

LABRADOR

QUEBEC

TADOUSSAC

TROIS-PISTOLES

St. Lawrence River

GASPÉ PENINSULA

GASPÉ

Percé Rock

Bonaventure Island

Anticosti

Island

Gulf of
St. Lawrence

St. Ge
B

Chaleur Bay

Miscou Island

BATHURST

NEW
BRUNSWICK

CHATHAM

Miramichi Bay

▽197 ft.

Magdalen
Islands

Cabot

PORT AUX BASQUES

Strait

MAINE

PRINCE EDWARD
ISLAND

PRINCE EDWARD ISLAND
NATIONAL PARK

CAPE BRETON
HIGHLANDS
NATIONAL PARK

CANADA
UNITED STATES

MONCTON

Hopewell
Rocks

FUNDY
NATIONAL
PARK

CHARLOTTETOWN

Cape Breton
Island

VERMONT

Kennebec River

Penobscot River

SAINT JOHN

Bay of Fundy

NEW GLASGOW

SYDNEY

Bras d'Or
Lake

Basque Island

NEW
HAMPSHIRE

Androscoggin River

Cadillac Mountain 1,530 ft.
Acadia Mountain 681 ft.

ACADIA
NATIONAL
PARK

MACHIASPORT

QUODDY HEAD

Grand Manan Island

Kent Island

NOVA   SCOTIA

HALIFAX

HACKETTS COVE

TOPSHAM
BRUNSWICK
PEMAQUID POINT

CASTINE
NEWCASTLE

BAR HARBOR

Frenchman Bay

Mount Desert Island

Somes Sound

Swan's Island

DIGBY
NECK

KEJIMKUJIK
NATIONAL PARK

PORTLAND

Casco
Bay

Muscongus
Bay

The Basin

FRENCHBORO

Burnt Coat Harbor

Hog Island

Monhegan Island

Matinicus Island

Isle au Haut

LIVERPOOL

Androscoggin River

KITTERY POINT

Vinalhaven
Island

MASSACHUSETTS

BOSTON

Gulf of Maine

▽813 ft.

Sable Island

The Northeast coast, as defined in this book and located by the blue rectangle at right, embraces shores and waters stretching from the northern tip of Newfoundland to Massachusetts, and from the St. Lawrence River eastward to the Grand Banks. This rockbound region is detailed in the relief map below, with the areas discussed in the text highlighted in green. The offshore waters are shown in shades of blue: the darker the shade, the deeper the water. On land, red outlines and red type are used to identify the region's six national parks. Solid black lines represent roads, and broken black lines trace state and national boundaries. Black dots mark towns and cities, while black squares indicate points of special interest discussed in the text.

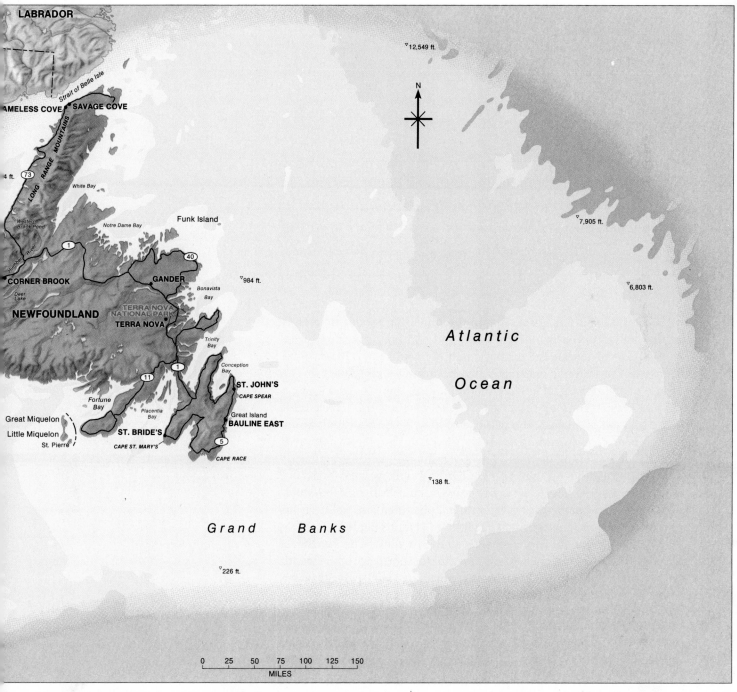

LABRADOR

Strait of Belle Isle

AMELESS COVE   **SAVAGE COVE**

LONG RANGE MOUNTAINS

4 ft.   73

White Bay

Western Brook Pond

Notre Dame Bay

Funk Island

1

40

Humber River

CORNER BROOK

Deer Lake

NEWFOUNDLAND

GANDER

Bonavista Bay

TERRA NOVA NATIONAL PARK

TERRA NOVA

▽ 984 ft.

Trinity Bay

1

11

Conception Bay

ST. JOHN'S

CAPE SPEAR

Fortune Bay

Placentia Bay

Great Island
BAULINE EAST

Great Miquelon

Little Miquelon

St. Pierre

ST. BRIDE'S

CAPE ST. MARY'S

5

CAPE RACE

▽ 12,549 ft.

N

▽ 7,905 ft.

▽ 6,803 ft.

Atlantic

Ocean

▽ 138 ft.

Grand   Banks

▽ 226 ft.

0   25   50   75   100   125   150
MILES

1/ The Drowned Shore

The river is within us, the sea is all about us;/The sea is the land's edge also, the granite/Into which it reaches, the beaches where it tosses/Its hints of earlier and other creation.... T. S. ELIOT/ THE DRY SALVAGES

Forget Boston. Head northeast. Ignore the unending sprout of motels along the highway, the fried-clam bars, the Leaning Tower of Pizza. Close your eye to the sludge oozing down the Merrimack River. Shut your nose to the spew of chemicals that is turning other rivers up the coast into dead streams—the Saco, the Kennebec, the Penobscot. Say a prayer for the millions of sea birds that once called this coast their own, the billions of salmon, the trillions of alewives. Don't look at the aluminum beer cans twinkling on every mud flat, the plastic detergent bottles that come sailing in on the tide like miniature white armadas.

Set your jaw against all this. You are fighting your way eastward out of an urban mess that has been slowly growing since Miles Standish arrived, an area that has been generally raped, poisoned and polluted for more than 300 years. The wonder is that there is anything left.

Keep going. Miraculously, there *is* something left. The Northeast coast of North America from Maine to the southern tip of Labrador —that part of our continent that has supported a constantly growing, constantly exploiting population of white men for longer than any other place in the Western Hemisphere—is still alive and well. Within a two-hour drive of Boston the alert traveler will begin to find patches of untouched wilderness, a bit of salt marsh, a fine stand of birch and maple, a wrinkled stretch of rocky shore with its attendant little coves and tidal pools that the paper mill, the bulldozer and the oil slick have bypassed. The American wilderness, that unbelievable, unending natural resource, was first dented along this coast. The coastal barrier is scratched and bent now, but it survives.

This book is about that coast. *Coast*—I repeat the word to impress on the reader that as he makes the journey vicariously he must imagine one foot always on dry land and the other in salt water; the area he will be asked to examine is extremely narrow. Unlike many seacoasts around the world, the transition here from continental forest to salt water is abrupt. The shoreline is mostly rock of an extremely durable variety, and it is wooded right to the water's edge. There are no deltas, few wide sweeps of sand and dune, no great expanses of swamp—nothing, in fact, to warn the visitor from inland that he may be approaching the sea. He can walk along a forest path for an hour and not know if he is one mile or 50 miles from the sea. Suddenly there will be a new whiff in the aromatic piny air, a sharp sea smell of kelp on wet rock, a rush and a low boom of nearby surf. A dozen steps more—and the trees end. Beyond them is bare rock. Beyond that the ocean.

How quick, and how dramatic. It is because of this extraordinary suddenness of change from forest to sea that a book about this coast need concern itself only with a ribbon of shoreline that is never more than a mile or two wide and is usually much less.

The length of the ribbon? As the crow flies, it is about a thousand miles from southern Maine to the nearest corner of Labrador. As a man walks, it is so much farther as to be comical. The Maine coast alone from Kittery Point to Quoddy Head (230 miles for the crow) would extend, for a man who conscientiously skirted every cove, rounded every headland and swam every river, over 3,000 miles. If he kept walking, up the Bay of Fundy and back down the other side, all around Nova Scotia, in and out of Chaleur Bay, around the Gaspé Peninsula and ended up by circumambulating Newfoundland, he would have walked—if he lived long enough and had the stamina to do it—some 25,000 miles. About once around the earth.

That difference, the fantastic discrepancy between crow flight and man walk, is caused by a fundamental characteristic of the Northeast coast. It is what is known as a "drowned coast." During four recent ice ages it was covered by glaciers that are estimated to have been between one and two miles thick. Since a single acre of ice a mile thick weighs almost seven million tons, it is not hard to understand how the entire land mass was pressed down by the glacier. And because the surface of the earth is very elastic, the coast can be expected to spring back again now that the ice is gone. But it has only partially done so, for these things take time—and there has been very little time since the ice left, a mere 14,000 years. Instead, all the water that had been locked up in the glacier melted and ran into the sea, raising its level by some 400 feet. It is this combination of depressed land and raised sea level that produces a drowned coast. River valleys that were once quite distant from the sea become fjords and bays. And all the little hills that are big enough to stick up above the invading sea become islands.

For me, this is not so much a drowned coast as it is *the* drowned coast of the world. Take a look at all those long arms of the sea reaching up into Casco Bay and Muscongus Bay, the endless wrinkles that indent Nova Scotia and Newfoundland. And the islands—Maine alone can boast more than a thousand, one of the thickest sprinklings anywhere. They are all made of rock, and nearly all of them have dense evergreen covers of their own, miniature replicas of the forests on the nearby mainland. In this way the forest invades the sea along the Northeast coast; the sea replies by penetrating deeply into the land. Everywhere the two go hand in hand.

Since the coast is made of rock, if we are to study it we must first study these rocks, remembering that much of the land has been scraped clean, gouged and scratched by glaciers. That will make study easy in one way because it will reveal some very ancient structures. But it will also complicate things because glaciers have the habit of carrying debris with them, and when they melt they often leave behind them rocks of all sizes that they may have picked up almost 200 miles away.

Thus the large boulder perched atop a cliff may bear no resemblance to the rock it is sitting on. Moreover, it may be considerably older. There is a tendency to assume that something sitting on something else arrived later and is therefore younger. As far as rocks are concerned, this is not necessarily so. The story of geology is one of constant change and movement in rocks. What was once molten magma deep in the earth can emerge as lava and harden into a mountain. Give or take a hundred million years and the mountain peak may find itself at the bottom of the sea, now in the form of sand or clay and slowly being transmuted by heat and by subterranean pressures into another kind of rock entirely, only to be thrust into the air once more by a wrinkling of the earth's surface. Round and round the process goes.

This endless cycle of change in rock has been going on since the first rains fell and the first seas were formed to receive continental sediments. The first mountain ever born automatically became the first to begin to die. When or where it was born will never be known. All that science can be sure of is that it took place prior to three billion years ago —for that is the age of the oldest known rocks in the world.

Most conveniently, the story of the Northeast coast starts here, at the very beginning of observable geological processes, because part of the coast is made up of some of the oldest rock, known as Precambrian rock. More importantly, much of its subsequent history has been affected by the existence, inland, of an enormous supply of it.

That huge supply is known as the Canadian shield, a vast expanse consisting mostly of tough granite that has covered large sections of central and eastern Canada for at least a billion years. What remains exposed is presumably the roots of mountain ranges worn down through ages of erosion to the relatively flat shield shape that is present now. Excluding Greenland, it covers 1,864,000 square miles. All of Labrador is made of Precambrian rock, as is one third of Newfoundland.

Not much is known about events during the Precambrian period. By contrast, for the period since, geologists can speak with more assurance. The endless processes of mountain building and decay, the birth and death of volcanoes, the laying down of deposits in vanished seas —all these begin to reveal themselves with increasing clarity the closer we come to the present. Different periods begin to assume their own distinct characteristics: they are given names and dates, and an actual history of the last half billion years of the earth's crust emerges. Chapters in that history may be read today in the rocks of the Northeast coast. It is a fascinating story. It reveals, for example, that Maine was once a land of volcanoes, that the present coastal area was actually sea bottom a good deal of the time, and that an enormous mountain range, comparable to the Rockies in size, had its birth here—and is now dying.

What causes mountains to grow and the earth's crust to wrinkle is still not clearly understood. But that these things happen is evident throughout the world. One testimony to the heaving and uprearing that takes place is the steep slants of rock that can be seen on Mount Desert Island in Maine, together with the effects of the recent ice ages.

My own introduction to the story of Maine's rock and ice came at Mount Desert a few summers ago during a cruise up the coast in a small auxiliary sloop. Sailing into Somes Sound, a narrow arm of the sea with steep rock cliffs rising on both sides, I anchored in a cove and my children and I went ashore to collect a bucket of mussels for supper and climb Acadia Mountain, which soars almost straight out of the water on the west side of the sound. Except for its dramatic steepness on its water side, Acadia is not much of a mountain. It is not quite 700 feet high, less than half the height of Mount Cadillac across the sound. The path to the summit is an easy one. It winds up through patches of blueberry and small gnarled conifers, around weathered granite slabs, and emerges in a jumble of bare broken rock at the top.

It was only when I reached the summit and looked around that the special quality of Acadia Mountain hit me. Its very steepness makes it seem much higher than it really is. My boat appeared to be almost directly under my feet, its handkerchief sails neatly furled, its mast pricking up like a matchstick—a toy in a bathtub. As I watched it, it began to drift slowly out into the middle of the sound. I focused my binoculars, and could see my wife scrambling to get the anchor up and the engine started. She had agreed to stay on board in case this might happen, for the wall of rock that rises from the sound to make the mountain continues on down just as steeply beneath the surface. Fifty feet from shore the water is 50 feet deep, and on a slant like that it is extremely difficult to get an anchor to hold. Out in the middle of the sound the bottom drops away to over 150 feet, a remarkable depth for such a narrow waterway. This great depth reminded me of something I had once been told: Somes Sound, once a river valley, was reshaped by a glacier and flooded by the sea. That makes it a true fjord, like those in Norway.

This meant that the trench below me had been dug by an unbelievable mass of ice slowly crunching its way to the sea between the little mountain on which I stood and the larger one across the way. More than that, the ice had not only gone between the mountains but had flowed right over their tops, suffocating them completely. On some forgotten frigid morning, far above where I now stood, if there had been any bird or other living presence to look about in the blinding light of an endless ice landscape, what sign could it have been given that there was an entire little mountain down below, crushed under the weight of ice? What staggered me was that the top of Acadia Mountain had been perhaps a mile beneath the surface of that gleaming, jagged ice field; that the view now spreading before me, reaching to the very rim of the horizon, had been similarly buried; and that the front of that fantastic wedge of ice, where prodigious hunks broke off and floated free, had been far to the east, out of sight over the curve of the earth.

"Don't leave me like that again," my wife said when we got down the mountain and back on board. "I mightn't have been able to start the engine." I couldn't answer. I began to clean the mussels, silenced for once by the sudden image I had had of all that ice.

In terms of geological time, the glacier departed only yesterday, leaving the land almost exactly as it may now be seen from such eminences as Acadia Mountain. In that respect the coast is a paradox: it is made of some very ancient rock, yet it is itself new.

The one thing that has changed since the ice left is vegetation. At first, of course, there wasn't any, nor any topsoil either; both had been scoured away. Where the land began to appear again along the edges of the shrinking ice sheet, there was nothing but raw rock or piles of stony debris and mud. This may have happened first along the coast, but most probably the first land to reappear was the tops of mountains, emerging where the ice had been thinnest. Gradually the great glacier became broken up into separate pieces, stranded blocks of ice that squatted immobile in the valleys for centuries until they too melted at last. And as long as there were still large amounts of ice lying about, the local climate was undoubtedly somewhat colder than it is now. As a result, the first things that could begin repopulating the land were lichens, mosses and other cold-tolerant low plants that could eke out a living in the barren soil. These were soon followed by a rapid recolonization by coniferous forest. The Northeast coast is ideal for conifers. They appreciate the damp that proximity to the sea brings. They do not mind the cold, they can survive a rather short growing season, and they can get by on poor soil. Thus, they have been the dominant trees along most of the coast since the forest returned.

The weather that these coastal conifers must endure varies from reasonably benign to absolutely atrocious. In Maine, as in most parts of the world, the sea has an ameliorating effect on the land. Water, with its tremendous capacity for heat storage, changes its temperature very slowly—and very little—compared to air. Thus it tends to level off extremes of heat and cold in the adjacent land; consequently many spots in inland Maine have far colder winters and hotter summers than its coastal islands.

To the east and north, however, the situation changes. The Labrador and Newfoundland coasts can be abominable places. The winter storms are ferocious and they sometimes blow for weeks, with temperatures dropping as far as 60° below zero in Labrador. The bays freeze solid and the pack ice grinds its way up and down the coast under the scourge of terrible winds. Even in summertime immense icebergs calved by the still-surviving Greenland icecap sail down the coast in a steady procession and are occasionally seen south of Halifax even as late as July.

The differences in climate along the Northeast coast are caused by ocean currents. Coming from the Arctic, and flowing down a long channel between Greenland and the Canadian mainland, is a vast flood of icy water known as the Labrador Current. This is the single most important influence on the Northeast coast. It perpetuates a cold climate for the cold-adapted vegetation that is there now. More, it has a profound influence on the animal life, both on land and in the water.

For animal life, the important thing about the Labrador Current is not so much that it is cold but that it is extremely rich in mineral nutrients that it picks up at the bottom of the polar sea. This richness supports a fantastic population of free-floating microscopic one-celled plants, which in turn provide food for an immense number of larger but still microscopic animals. These are eaten by still larger animals, and so on up the scale to good-sized fish, which in their turn are eaten by seals and the seals by killer whales or men. This is a classic food chain. Of the many such chains that exist the world over, it is one of the most dramatic because of its great number of intermediate steps, and because its end product is so much larger and scarcer than the things that go to make up the base. How many specks of individual plankton, each a complete plant or animal in itself, it takes to support one seal-eating whale may never be calculated, but it is surely up in the trillions of trillions, a figure so large as to strain the imagination.

Even some of the intermediate steps in the chain produce staggering populations—or did before their decimation by man. Lobsters, for instance, used to be incredibly abundant. Sometimes storms carried them ashore in such numbers that the early colonists would collect them in wagonloads for use as fertilizer. As for the cod, they lay like a living carpet over thousands of square miles of ocean bottom.

On land the richness of life, though it did not compare with the marine population, was still spectacularly impressive, particularly because it was all there in full view. Seals were abundant everywhere. Walruses, now reduced to a few pitiful little colonies in some of the remotest areas of the Arctic, once thronged the coasts of Newfoundland, Nova Scotia and Maine, and were known as far south as Massachusetts. But what must have most stunned the credulity of pioneer sealers and fishermen was the unbelievable abundance of certain species of sea birds that nested (and in a few places still do) in rocky seagirt cliffs and ledges where predators could not get at them. Some offshore islands sustained populations running into the millions.

South of Newfoundland and off the Nova Scotia coast, the Labrador Current meets another gigantic oceanic influence, the Gulf Stream, and is dragged out to sea by it. This plus the gradual warming of the current itself as it works south explains why the weather on the Maine coast is so much more benign than that of Newfoundland and Labrador. It also accounts for the last large-scale phenomenon of the area: fog.

When the warm moisture-laden air riding north over the Gulf Stream hits the cold water riding down on the Labrador Current, the water vapor in the air condenses into a thick fogbank that stands off the coast like a dirty gray curtain, day after day, week after week. Sometimes it gets blown out to sea so that for a day all the world is a miracle of clarity and bright sparkle, with every last island etched sharp against the blue sky as far as the eye can see. But the wind will change, the fogbank will creep closer and closer to the land, and soon the outer islands of Maine —Swan's, Isle au Haut, Matinicus, Monhegan—are blotted out. People may continue to go on sunny picnics and improve their tans farther up the bays, in Castine or the resorts at the head of Casco Bay, but 10 miles away, off in the islands, one can be lost for two or three weeks on end in a pearly swirl and drip that is another world entirely. Just east of Swan's Island lies another smaller island with one tiny fishing village on it, Frenchboro. A path runs for half a mile through pine woods from the village across the island to its outer beach. Walking there in a dense fog, with even denser streams floating past like swirls of milk being stirred into a glass of already milky water, unable to see beyond that looming boulder 50 yards ahead or those twin spruces spiking up behind —with the world always changing as you walk because of the smallness of your vision—you can feel as lost and remote from modern civilization as it is possible to be within the continental United States. The round rocks gleam like polished marble in the wet; the kelp sucks and sways in the tide. You are totally alone. After two minutes your hair and eyebrows are beaded with droplets that soon cover your sweater like a cobweb freighted with dew. Two minutes more and you can wring the water from the wool. A lone sandpiper flits along ahead of you like a tiny ghost, picking busily among the pebbles. Offshore a seal may poke up his head to stare at you briefly. Somewhere a distant foghorn may be grunting. Otherwise nothing.

In such a place and at such a time, who needs the sun?

Since the influence of northern water is stronger the farther northeast one goes, it is also increasingly foggy in that direction. According to the

National Weather Service, one may expect 25 days of fog a year in Kittery Point and 50 to 60 in Portland, Bar Harbor and Machiasport. In some parts of Newfoundland it is foggy practically all the time—when it is not snowing. But even in Newfoundland go a few miles inland and it is clear again. The fog can be a terrible nuisance for the fisherman, or the lobsterman who has to tend his pots in all weather. They have to ghost along among the unseen islands and ledges, feeling their way about, and they do, with uncanny skill—as does the experienced yachtsman, for whom these coastal waters offer the most interesting and unspoiled cruising in North America.

Despite the care it imposes on sailors, fog is a boon overall. It provides a steady supply of moisture for coastal vegetation. And the floor of the woodland that edges the sea responds magnificently. It is a wonderland of fragrant green stuff, springy underfoot, a delight to walk on. All along the coast, and in Maine in particular, the choicest wilderness spots seem to be on its small islands. That is entirely proper, for wilderness need not be large, only undisturbed. Islands, thanks to the very inconvenience of reaching them, have a magic of their own that anybody who has lived for any time on an island will know, and under whose spell even the casual visitor can quickly fall. A woodland walk on the mainland, while often longer and more varied than is possible on any of the small Maine islands, somehow lacks the sense of enchantment of an island walk.

For such a taste of the coastal woodland, Hog Island in Muscongus Bay boasts a fine stand of red and white spruce, birch and balsam fir. The island is less than two miles long, but the path running through it is much longer. It winds among the trees, edges the shore, skirts a pretty little marsh, and offers so many delights to the visitor that he can spend a day there, and go back for another walk tomorrow. Not far from Hog Island is another little island paradise *(pages 44-57)*.

An even shorter walk—but such a gem that no one who takes it will ever forget it—is on Vinalhaven Island in Penobscot Bay. It skirts an almost completely landlocked cove called the Basin, a circular depression not quite half a mile across, dotted with one- and two-tree islets and filled with outcrops of rock, water smoothed, ancient and yellow. Its entrance is scarcely more than 20 feet across, and through this narrow sluice millions of gallons of water must pass four times a day on the changes of the tide. When the current is at its height it whirls through so fast that it is impossible to row against. On the bottom, bits of weed go spinning past, together with hermit crabs bouncing along like acorns in their rented shells, and an occasional little blueclaw desperately paddling. Meanwhile, inside the Basin, the rising water whispers up the rocks and sunning seals lurch clumsily higher. Small periwinkles, sprinkled like gravel and glued shut against the air, open up and begin to move again as the healing water closes over them. There is a subdued rustle everywhere, as of life on the move. Minute rafts of sand, lifted ever so gently, float away intact, only to disintegrate at the touch of a ripple. Finally the great tub is full and sits motionless for half an hour on the flood. A few gulls sleep on the rocks. Their time to stir will come when all that water slides out again, exposing all the little living things.

The Basin is an exquisite tidal jewel, made more exquisite by being mounted in a woodland setting that displays it to perfection. To reach it from the nearest road is a walk of only a few hundred yards across a field. The path that opens ahead of you will bring you to the Basin's edge, and you can follow it along, with the water on your right, for no more than half a mile until you reach the sluice gate at its mouth.

A short walk, but lined with what a richness of mosses and ferns —cinnamon and bracken—and beds of blue flag, wild roses and huckleberries. As you walk, vignettes of the Basin will open up through the trees—if you can bear to lift your eyes from the fantastic miniature forests of club moss, ground cedar and clover at your feet, or stop looking at the great blue heron or the osprey flapping by. When you have picked your fill of chanterelle mushrooms for supper and wandered down to the water a couple of times for a better view of the seals from a projecting rocky point, you will find yourself at the end of the path, approaching the back door of somebody's house—somebody who surely lives in one of the earth's enchanted spots. Clamp down on your envy and walk back to your car, thankful that you have at least been introduced to the place, if you cannot live there yourself.

For me the essence of the Northeast coast lies in Vinalhaven's Basin. Mammal, bird and marine life meet there. The miracle of the tides affects all life with its rhythm. It is a place of the sea, and yet it is surrounded by forest—and all of it embedded in the old rock that gives the entire coast its character.

Chronicles in Stone

PHOTOGRAPHS BY JOHN DE VISSER

Most people correctly think of the Northeast coast as a stretch of rock. But relatively few are aware that, from the islanded bays of Maine to the mountains of Newfoundland, the rock takes a tremendous variety of forms, and that its history is a fascinating reflection of the geological past of the continent itself.

Over hundreds of millions of years the continent has been subjected to forces of stress and strain, generated in the interior of the earth, that lifted and crumpled many of its plains to form mountains. It has also been subjected to the less violent surface forces of wind and water that wore the peaks down to form new plains. All these processes are apparent, for example, in the eroded mountains of Newfoundland, the northeastern terminus of the ancient system of ranges called the Appalachians.

While mountains rose and fell, molten materials welled up in huge bulges that solidified below the surface into the granitic rocks seen in Maine and throughout the Northeast. Some of the molten material also erupted above the surface, spewing lava that hardened to form the basalt columns of Nova Scotia. In many areas, this igneous material has lain for millennia under invading seas while grains of silt from rivers and the corpses of sea creatures settled to the bottom to build up layers of sediment. The resulting mud, sand and lime, thousands of feet thick, hardened into shale, sandstone and limestone formations like those of New Brunswick.

Glaciers, too, have shaped the Northeast coast, scraping and chiseling the land and causing it to subside slowly under their enormous weight. And at all times and places on the coast, the ocean waves and tides have been ceaselessly at work, changing the shoreline.

Only a few yards inland, the geological record is concealed by soil and vegetation. But where the sea meets the land and erosion has laid bare the rocks, the story, outlined in the pictures on the following pages, is clearly legible.

To the careful observer the rocks reveal more about coastal land forms than merely their beauty. Their story makes it possible to imagine the land as it looked millions of years ago; the islands poking through Frenchman Bay in the picture at right would loom as peaks, with valleys between them where the sea now glimmers, and with ridges receding over the horizon.

The shore at Mount Desert Island in Maine shows several effects of glaciation. The coastline, pushed down some 40,000 years ago by the weight of a glacier, is still depressed so that the sea flows into both Frenchman Bay (background) and the cove in the foreground. The steep cliff at top left is the result of "plucking"—the removal of large chunks of rock by the ice sheet as it moved past on its way to the sea.

Basalt columns (left) at Digby Neck in the Bay of Fundy resulted from the cooling of lava, part of a huge flow of igneous rock that burst through existing layers of sedimentary rock on the west coast of Nova Scotia and covered them to a thickness of 875 feet. The lava cooled rapidly, hardening into the columnar shapes shown. Subsequently, they were buried under soft sedimentary rock, but now, 175 million years later, this sediment has been eroded away, leaving the columns exposed to frost and sea, as well as to penetration by trees. Growing in the soil that collects in the rock crevices, the trees slowly widen the cracks, breaking up the columns one by one.

Resembling abstract sculpture, Hopewell Rocks in New Brunswick are on the opposite side of the Bay of Fundy from the columns at left. They are 100 million years older but much softer, consisting of reddish gravels washed from ancient mountain ranges, buried by later deposits and compacted into the rough conglomerate shown here. Now they are exposed to weathering and to Fundy's powerful tides. Where the rock faces are weakest —along fracture lines—the waves carve out caves, then cut arches through them. Eventually the arches fall in, leaving isolated stacks. These, too, will topple as the waves eat away at their necks. But since the red conglomerate extends inland for 1,000 feet, new caves, arches and stacks are continually being formed.

Nestling in the Gulf of St. Lawrence, Prince Edward Island, Canada's smallest province, has a very different look from that of the shores of Nova Scotia, New Brunswick and Maine. The older rocks seen in those regions are here overlaid by a sedimentary deposit formed by sand washed from ancient mountains inland and accumulated as shale and sandstone. This deposit is what makes the surface of Prince Edward today (the red color comes from iron oxide). As in New Brunswick, the waves eat at the soft surface material, but with a different result. There the high tides and swift currents carry away material as fast as it is washed loose, leaving the many bizarre forms shown on the previous page. At Prince Edward, however, tides are small and the surrounding waters very shallow. Thus any material that the waves dislodge by undercutting the cliffs is washed up and down the shore, grinding itself smaller and smaller in the process, and producing some of the finest sand beaches in all Canada.

Percé Rock, noted for its arch and its stack formation, looms like an architectural ruin out of the sea off the Gaspé Peninsula. The rock, like those in the foreground—splashed with runoff from a small waterfall—is the weathered remnant of an ancient mountain. It consists of limestone laid down in thin horizontal layers on a sea bed about 375 million years ago, but lying vertically today as a result of mountain-building upheavals in the earth. Now starkly exposed to the elements, Percé Rock is disappearing fast, as geological time is reckoned.

Three hundred years ago sailors counted four arches in it. All traces of two of these—at the seaward end—are gone. The third collapsed in 1845, leaving only a small stack (far right).

The remaining arch is now being enlarged by wave action. In all, Percé Rock is being eaten away at a rate of 300 tons a year, and will be consumed entirely in another 13,000 years.

The Long Range Mountains of northwestern Newfoundland, seen here across a tundra bog, look like the building blocks of some prehistoric

giant. Their level tops are the surface of a peneplain, an area that was worn flat by ancient rivers, then uplifted about 60 million years ago.

2/ Forests on the Move

There was a fine view of the harbor and its long stretches of shore all covered by the great army of the pointed firs, darkly cloaked and standing as if they waited to embark. Among the outer islands, the trees seemed to march seaward still, going steadily over the heights and down to the water's edge. SARAH ORNE JEWETT/ THE COUNTRY OF THE POINTED FIRS

For the trees of the Northeast coast the event that more than any other shaped their destiny was the end of the last ice age, 14,000 years ago. As the glacier retreated from North America, leaving behind a lifeless landscape of sterile mud and stones, it also left a great deal of water. A world just emerging from the grip of an ice sheet is a very soggy one. Depressions and troughs gouged in the land become lakes; drifts of deposited debris often become dams. Large isolated blocks of ice that have been buried in mud and gravel will endure for centuries, insulated against melting just as a block of ice in an icehouse is insulated by sawdust. The Northeast was strewn with such leftover giant ice cubes. When they finally melted, many left behind them hollows in the ground that became ponds.

Neither lakes nor ponds are permanent features of a landscape. Lake beds fill with sediment carried there by streams. Natural dams break down and the water flows away. Gradually the lakes become shallower, turn to marshland and over many centuries dry out completely. Ponds have even shorter lives. Connecticut today, having been freed from the ice longer, is not nearly as wet as Maine, which in turn has dried out more than Newfoundland. But there is still a tremendous amount of water in the Northeast, as I noted when I flew recently from

Massachusetts to Saint John, New Brunswick. The multitude of lakes and ponds gleaming below me was astonishing. These increased as I flew north and east, giving me the impression that I was moving back through time, getting closer and closer to the conditions that followed the ice age, as indeed I was.

When the glacier finally began its retreat, exposing the waterlogged land beneath, the first plants to return—the lichens, mosses and sedges —began to create an environment of sorts. They helped hold the sterile glacial rubble in place, thus slowing down erosion, and also contributed small amounts of organic richness to the soil. In time shrubs moved in, and ultimately trees.

A similar pattern is followed today on any piece of forest land cleared by man or fire, where the returning vegetation tends to go through certain phases. The first plants to appear will be very small ones, followed by shrubs, then quick-growing sun-loving trees. The last to appear will be shade-tolerant trees that can only develop in the shadow of the earlier colonists. Hemlock, for example, will slowly assert itself in groves of oak and maple and will ultimately crowd them out. In the deep shade of a mature hemlock grove only other hemlocks will flourish. A forest that has reached this state of stability is called a climax forest. Such forests once cloaked much of the Northeast, and a few tracts of climax forest may still be found there, but they are not always dominated by the same kind of trees that asserted themselves after the ice melted.

Since trees cannot move about and since most of them live longer than most men, we tend to assume that mature forests are immutable things. They seem to have been standing for ages where we find them standing now. There is even a sense of permanence in the idea of a "climax" forest, which seems susceptible only to the threats of fire and the ax. These threats, we assume, do not really change the forest since the individual trees that are burned or cut down will be replaced by young trees of the same type.

Nothing could be more wrong than our impression of permanence. Although individual trees cannot move, entire forests can. They parade up and down the continents under the goad of climatic change, and as they come and go they often change their character too with new types of vegetation replacing what was there before. Forests are on the move right now in response to gradual changes in the climate, but this is taking place so slowly that we do not notice it.

In postglacial times, as the climate of the Northeast warmed up somewhat, a condition was reached under which two kinds of trees could establish dominance: spruce and balsam fir. Both of these conifers are hardy fast-growing types that can get a foothold in poor soil. They thrive in damp cold climates, as do willow, birch, poplar and tamarack. The willow and tamarack like it wettest and are found in increasing abundance in spongy, boggy land the farther north one goes. The birch and poplar prefer it somewhat drier. But the spruce and balsam seem to do well everywhere; we can assume that they once prospered mightily throughout the Northeast. But as conditions have become warmer and drier even they have dwindled. Now they are truly dominant only at or near the sea. For their persistence there we can thank the Labrador Current. What we are looking at today as we make our way north and east is a forest left over from an earlier postglacial past, saved from engulfment by oak, beech, maple, hemlock—a host of species that have become dominant elsewhere—by a cold climate perpetuated by frigid water flowing from the polar sea.

Despite this climatic assist we must give the spruce and the fir some credit for their tenacity. Once established they are hard to dislodge. Both grow rapidly and extremely densely. Like most conifers, they need a minimum of nourishment from the soil, and instead of enriching it by the deposition of loam as a deciduous forest slowly will, they have their own peculiar—and self-perpetuating—effect on it. The carpet of needles that they drop is strongly acid in character. This acid seeps into the ground and gradually reacts with the minerals in the pulverized granite that makes up most of the soil in the Northeast. In time everything but quartz is dissolved, leaving a fine whitish-gray sand that has no chemical nourishment in it at all. This is a poor environment for other trees. Barring catastrophes, the spruce-fir forest endures unchallenged even though it may be living on borrowed time toward the southern end of its range.

There *are* catastrophes. Diseases like the spruce budworm have in the past killed great tracts of spruce forest. Hurricanes cause immense blowdowns. Fires not only utterly consume these highly combustible trees but also burn up whatever forest litter they have laboriously been husbanding. Mount Desert Island on the Maine coast was the victim of a bad fire nearly 25 years ago, one that burned off about 10,000 acres of spruce-fir forest. This, and subsequent erosion of the bare soil, so denuded the steeper slopes of the island that for a number of years nothing grew there except blueberry bushes, wild flowers and some small ground-covering plants. These were eventually followed by varieties of birch and other trees like sumac and poplar that do well in thin or burned-over soil.

It will be interesting to see what finally happens on Mount Desert Island. It is warmer and drier there now than when the spruce first came. If the birches enrich the soil enough for the establishment of other long-lived hardwoods, their leafy branches would block the sun and there would not be enough light for spruce and fir to become dominant. However, there are young spruces and firs springing up there right now. What kind of a climax forest will eventually prevail is a question that cannot yet be answered.

Right now there are several different kinds of coastal forest. An inland climax of oak and hickory has broken through to the sea in southern Maine. Whether or not these trees can work their way farther northward will depend on long-range temperature trends, and nobody can yet say whether the climate is getting colder or warmer. During the last 500 years it has done a little of both. If the climate should get warmer and drier there could be a northward invasion of pitch pines, the dominant tree of Cape Cod and sandy southern Massachusetts. If it should get colder and wetter, then white spruce and balsam could come marching down where they are unknown today. On their heels would be the tamarack and black spruce of Newfoundland's bogs.

Thinking about trees creates an impatience in man. His life is too short; he wishes time could be condensed so that he could see the outcome of the slow forest processes unfolding all around him—not to mention their effect on all the small things that grow beneath them and change with them. These are far more varied than the trees and are worth a lifetime of study themselves. The following pages give a glimpse at some of the lesser plants that—at this particular moment in slow time—share the Northeast coast with the dominant spruce and fir.

A Wilderness Reborn

PHOTOGRAPHS BY SONJA BULLATY AND ANGELO LOMEO

The essence of the Northeast coast is its islands, those small forested humps that sprinkle it from one end to the other. Each is unique, but all are alike in that their most important natural attributes are about the same. The problem for me was: which, among thousands, to choose to give the reader a concentrated view of one spot that speaks for the entire region—to offer him a close-in look at the things that make *this* wilderness what it is.

My choice was resolved by the owner of an island in Maine's Muscongus Bay who gave me permission to visit it with Christopher Packard, a botanist. The island is ideal for a nature walk. Comprising only a hundred acres, it is small enough to be thoroughly explored in a day, but rich enough in its variety to interest a naturalist for much longer than that. One particularly interesting aspect of the island is that it was cleared of its trees sometime in the past. Sheep were grazed there for a few years, but since then the wilderness has been allowed to follow the natural processes of return, the various stages of which are visible right now in different parts of the island. Finally, the island is far enough offshore to have a long fetch of open

water to the southwest. The result is an exposed headland at one end, stark and often storm lashed, with an environment far more severe than that on the northeast side, which is protected by ledges and has quiet tidal water and a small beach. The vegetation in these two spots, though they are only a few hundred yards apart, is totally different.

I have not named the island because its owner asked me not to. He lives there in summer with his wife and family and knows that anything written about the place may attract visitors and imperil not only his privacy but the island's unspoiled, evolving wilderness.

The best way to experience the island is to emerge from the sea, as it were. There is a small dock on the protected side of the island, and the visitor can step from boat to dock and thence immediately to a small strip of typical Maine beach: a little coarse sand and a great many stones.

A Beach of Wrinkled Rock

The crudity and newness of this beach are accentuated by its appearing to have been dropped there almost absent-mindedly by the currents that swirl around the island; it lies cupped in a jagged reef of metamorphic rock that underlies this

The nature walk described here took place on a mile-and-a-half-long private island in Maine's Muscongus Bay. Landing on the island's protected eastern shore, the author came upon the stretch of metamorphic rock pictured at right, whose corduroylike ridges are the edges of layers upturned 350 million years ago. From this point, at right in the map below, he crossed the island to its windswept western shore—a distance of about half a mile.

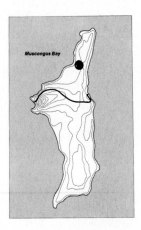

Muscongus Bay

THE ISLAND'S EASTERN SHORE, SHIELDED BY ROCK

The tide is fairly high as we come ashore and are met by the island's owner. We turn down the beach. To the left, in the tidal pools, is a gently moving world of brownish rockweed, to the right the beginnings of a tangle of land vegetation. In between is a curiosity: some green plants apparently growing in salt water. These are very conspicuous. Since the change from sea to land is a critical one, not many plants can survive in the region of transition, and any strip of beach at about the high-tide level is apt to be bare. Nevertheless, here are a few bold green tufts, their roots at the moment submerged in the shallow salt water, their stems stretching confidently to the sun. Two of these grow in small clusters: glasswort and sea blite. A third, orach, is a pretty plant that has red-streaked stems and leaves shaped like arrowheads. There is also a coarse grass here with a broad flat blade: cord grass. All flourish in this narrow environment that gives their roots a good soaking in salt water a couple of hours a day but permits them to live as dry-land plants the rest of the time. If they move farther up the beach they run into drier conditions and heavy competition from other types of plants, and cannot hold their own.

Just above high-tide level lichens begin to appear on the bare rock. These are the pioneers, the first plants to return to a denuded land. But the rock here reveals that there are pioneers among the pioneers —small, shapeless gray or black encrustations, some as broad as sil-

PIONEER PLANTS AT THE OCEAN'S EDGE

shore and pokes itself above the surface at intervals. The tumultuous geological past of the coast is written in this rock, which is hundreds of feet thick and composed of many narrow strata of contrasting materials. None of this structure would be visible except that some 350 million years ago the earth shuddered and brought the rock layer cake to the surface, heaving it up on edge so that the strata stick straight up along the island's eastern shore. A few yards inland the layers are covered with glacial deposits and topsoil, but here on the open shore they resemble a giant piece of corduroy, the softer seams more deeply eroded than the harder ones next to them.

GLASSWORT AT HIGH-TIDE MARK

ver dollars, others no thicker than a dime. These are crustose lichens, the flattest, toughest, slowest-growing, most unassuming lichens found on this island. They hunch so low that they are easily overlooked. They produce an acid that breaks down the rock into particles, and as they grow—and die—they trap minute amounts of their own organic detritus in their tiny wrinkled forms, along with wind-blown bits of dust. The result of these processes is the first faint flicker of soil formation. It alters the barren rock just enough for a second type, a yellow lichen, to establish itself. This is a little bigger, frillier and faster growing, and in turn provides a still richer environment for a still larger variety, parmelia, a rough green-gray foliose lichen that is extremely common along the shores of the island.

I turn away from the lichens toward the vastly more complex plants forming a green fringe on the upper edges of the beach only a few feet away. Here I encounter an abrupt change. This is a new stage with an entirely new cast of characters. The stage is a narrow one, fluctuating within a few feet from season to season. Its actors can grow just so close to the water because of the killing influence of the salt; the higher up the shore they move, the more competition they meet from other plants. The soil here is not good, but it is vastly more fertile than that of the beach itself. It supports several grasses, a thick growth of beach pea and such waste-ground plants as ragweed, curled dock and mullein with

ROCKWEED INVADING GRASS

SEASIDE GOLDENROD

A PARASITE: COMMON DODDER

its hairy leaves and tall central stalk.

With these tough, stringy colonizers is a very familiar plant but with a different look about it. Packard identifies it as seaside goldenrod, with rounder, smoother leaves than some roadside varieties. It is found only in this narrow habitat close to the sea: an intriguing example of evolutionary adaptation that makes it possible for one form of a plant to survive best where the soil is poor and the competition low, and others where the soil is richer and the competition more severe. Another plant found here is common dodder. It solves the soil problem by ignoring it. Dodder is a parasite; it puts forth no true roots but instead attaches itself to an existing weed by means of a net of orange stems that feed on —and may ultimately kill—its host.

Every step inland brings an enrichment of the soil and a corresponding enrichment of the vegetation, which grows in increasingly varied and luxuriant forms. The plants are bigger, too; they have to be in order to get up through their own tangle to the sun. For the first time since leaving the water's edge I begin to get a feeling, not of plants struggling against a harsh environment, but of plants struggling with each other. In this struggle more and more of the earth's water, its gases and chemicals are converted into tissue. Life has taken over, and is triumphantly represented in the clusters of daisies that sprout here, the sow thistles that look like superdandelions, the Canada thistles springing tall and straight. As I watch, a dragonfly, its transparent wings and jewellike colors scintillating in the sunlight, pauses to rest on a blade of the grass that grows thick near a bayberry bush.

Bayberry—a landmark! We have come only 50 feet from the water but what a profound change there has been in that short distance. What we have encountered so far has been grasses and weeds, plants that spring

A FEW STEPS FROM THE BEACH, PLANTS IN TANGLED COMPETITION

A DRAGONFLY IN THE SUN

up and die in a single season. Bayberry is a bush that survives for years. It has no hollow pulpy stem, but true branches made of wood. It has the structure and chemistry of a tree. It might even be called a tree except that it would never grow as tall as one. It grows in a dense tangle, shooting low-branching gnarled stems out of the ground everywhere.

The sun is warm here, back from the beach. Spicy smells waft from the shiny bayberry leaves and the drying grasses. I become conscious of berries. The bayberry, of course, has them, in tight clusters and colored a pale gray with bumpy surfaces like miniature golf balls. A patch of pasture juniper also has berries; the plant stands only a couple of feet high, with prickly, shaggy evergreen

BAYBERRIES ON A WOODY STALK

foliage, and bears hundreds of small blue-gray berries dusted with white. Martini drinkers can thank juniper berries for the flavor they give to gin.

But there are also berries here of a more immediate interest. There are strawberries, their prime unfortunately over now, in August, but what a crop there must have been in early July, dangling under all these green leaves spreading close to the ground. There are blackberries, just coming into season. How capriciously they do this. Here is a bush with some 50 berries on it, all but two of them small, red and hard. But the two exceptions are large and have miraculously turned purplish black. Why these two? And how is it that they are suddenly ripe while all the others are not? Will two more be ripe tomorrow? A dozen? All of them? I will not be here to find out. Gratefully I harvest the chosen two; they burst deliciously on my tongue.

The Bounty of a Berry Patch

There are also raspberries. The owner of the island has, from long residence, become a connoisseur of raspberries. "Don't waste your time on these low plants here. The tastiest berries are in those higher bushes up ahead where the spruce are just beginning to come in."

We walk a few yards more in the direction of a grove of spruce, and find ourselves swimming nearly up to our shoulders in raspberry bushes. The owner has cut a narrow path through them; elsewhere they are impenetrable. We stroll along, picking only the largest, deepest-colored berries. They literally drop into our hands and are as sweet and fragrant as any I have ever tasted. I sit down in the path to select a handful of the best. An enormous daddy longlegs climbs slowly and suspiciously over my foot and disappears in the thicket of raspberry canes.

Raspberries are a distinct stage in the evolving cycle of vegetation here. Like blackberries, they love sun, and when the land was cleared, a hundred or more years ago, the raspberry bushes had only to wait for the sheep to depart before making a comeback, gradually growing higher in their effort to outstrip one another. Where we stand now is what might be called a raspberry climax—the plants are as big and as dense as they will ever get. But their supremacy is an uneasy one and will

JUNIPER BERRIES ON SPIKY TWIGS

not last long. Just ahead loom the spruces, casting a deep shade that is certain death to raspberries. Around us, poking their heads up above the berry bushes like alert scouts, are young trees four or five feet tall, outriders from the spruce nation, reconnoitering new territory.

A hundred feet farther, and we are in the edge of the woods.

"When I came here twenty years ago," says our host, "this was a superb berry patch. There were no spruces here at all. There was a good stand of them at the south end of the island, and they have been coming this way ever since. I suppose if I do nothing they'll cover the island."

I look back through the trees, across several acres of berry bushes and toward his house. The house is

BLACKBERRIES, RIPENING RED AND RIPE DEEP PURPLE

in a small meadow that he keeps mowed. Beyond is another stretch of berry bushes, narrowing down to a point at the northern end of the island where herring gulls nest among the rocks and grasses. In my mind a swift shadow, like a gull's wing, passes over this bright landscape and coats it with spruces.

I ask, "Doesn't anything bother the spruces?"

"Yes, indeed," replies Packard. "Winter storms do, fires do, and

GOLDENROD AND PIONEER SPRUCE

—look here—this is one of their worst enemies."

I examine the spruce twig he is holding and see, hidden among the green needles, a dozen thin red spikes growing directly out of the twigs. I look further. The tree is covered with them.

"Dwarf mistletoe," says Packard. "A bad parasite. It's killing the tree." It obviously is. Its needles are

LICHEN-SPOTTED SPRUCE TRUNKS AND BRANCHES IN A FOREST MAZE

stunted and dry looking, nothing like the bursting rich greenness of a young spruce next to it.

"That stuff is all over the island," says the owner. "It's finishing off the trees up ahead at a great rate."

"Then how can the forest survive?" I ask.

"Because young trees keep springing up. They grow pretty big before they get infected."

We walk deeper into them, and within a dozen yards there is anoth-

branches are as vexatious and spiky as porcupine quills, again making walking difficult and encouraging us to stick to the path.

To our right, where a trickle of sunlight penetrates, is a lush bed of lady ferns. A wood nymph, a soft brown butterfly with lighter circles on its wings, flits slowly over the ferns and lights on a pale lavender wood aster. Its progress is languid and unafraid, quite unlike that of the more vigorous swallowtails, fritillar-

FILTERED SUNLIGHT ON A BED OF LADY FERNS

er dramatic change. We have entered a world of stillness, of dampness and dense shade. The spruces crowd so closely that their tops provide an uninterrupted canopy of green. Because scarcely any sunlight filters through, weeds and bushes are absent. The forest floor is indeed a floor, needle strewn and open except for the trunks of the trees and their silvery dead lower branches. The

ies and cabbage butterflies that live out in the sunny berry patches and meadows where marauding birds prey on them. Here few birds come. There is a flicker knocking on a dead trunk nearby as he excavates for wood-boring beetles and grubs, and a small party of chickadees and purple finches up in the treetops. Down here in the deep shade the wood nymph sails gently back and forth unmolested. Nymph is a perfect name for her. She recalls the old Greek belief that there were spirits in forest glades. When the flicker interrupts his drumming, it is so quiet here that the idea of a local presence seems quite believable. It is more than quiet; it is utterly still, like the velvet interior of a jewel box.

Velvet. That word jumps into my mind from somewhere. I look around me. The forest floor is carpeted with velvet—with moss.

Spruce woods, being uniformly shady and moist, are a paradise for mosses, mushrooms and lichens. I crouch to examine this small world that, from a few inches away, begins to reveal itself. My eye and mind make a rapid adjustment of scale, and I find myself entering a Lilliputian landscape of totally unexpected beauty and complexity. The longer I look, the more I see. In front of me is a forest of what appear to be minuscule pine trees, except that they grow with a uniformity and dense brilliant green that no pines could ever achieve—and they are only two inches high. This is haircap moss; along with the dusky golden spine fungus through which it grows, it restores my belief in elves, whom I half expect to see strolling in this miniature forest.

Beyond the haircap moss are a dozen round green tufts scattered here and there. They have the densest, most velvety texture of all, and the velvet curls down under their edges, giving the impression that they are not attached to the ground but are just sitting there. I pick one

HAIRCAP MOSS GROWING THROUGH A SPINE FUNGUS

A FOREST FLOORING OF SPRUCE CONES AND PINCUSHION MOSS

up. It *is* sitting there—no roots, no other attachment.

"It's exactly like a pincushion," I say in amazement.

"That's its name," says Packard.

The mosses are stunningly beautiful. Where a rare shaft of sun hits them they glow. And, like velvet in a jewel box, they have their own jewels to set off: mushrooms.

The Mushroom's Brief Splendor

There are mushrooms the color of rubies alongside amethyst-colored mushrooms and topaz-colored mushrooms like the golden *Laccaria laccata.* The mushrooms come singly, portly specimens with stalks an inch or two thick. They come in clusters, some so small that the feeblest elf could pluck one as an umbrella. They change shape with age—age being a matter of days in the headlong way mushrooms measure time. During the night an amanita mushroom will poke a bold round cap up through the spruce needles. The next day the cap will flatten out into the classic "toadstool" shape, then develop a dimple in its center deep enough to catch rain water, and a day or two later the once-beautiful mushroom begins to die a death of swift brown gooey deliquescence.

Mushrooms are fungi, as are the exquisite white plants at my feet. Called coral fungi, they resemble tiny spired castles or cathedrals carved in ivory. Also fungi are the semicircular shelflike growths that project from the trunks of some of the spruces. These are much woodier and more durable than ordinary mushrooms, and are smooth and whitish on their underside. I remember from my childhood that it is possible to scratch a message with a pointed stick or even a thumbnail in this smooth surface. Where it is scratched, the fungus will soon turn brown and the message will be clearly legible throughout the summer. I try the old trick once again: HELLO HELEN, addressed to my wife, who

MATURE: A LACCARIA LACCATA

unfortunately is on the mainland and cannot read it.

"We used to call these visiting cards," I say to Packard.

"They're also called 'artist's fungus,'" he replies, and then points to the bottom of the tree, where a two-inch cloud of foam appears to be suspended not far above the ground.

"That foamlike mold is a fungus," he says, "a fungus on a fungus. And it is parasitizing a mushroom. You can't see the mushroom inside the foam but it's there."

A few yards farther on there is a large spruce prostrate next to the path, dead long enough for damp and rot to blur its shape. Its wood is

AGING: A FLUTED AMANITA

punky, crumbly to the touch, full of spongy chasms; pieces have fallen off. Although inert now, long past the concern or influence of the wind, it is still a tree in motion, flowing almost visibly back into the earth. In another half-dozen years or so it will have become a burial mound, a

OLD–MAN'S–BEARD AND PARMELIA

shapeless hump in the forest no longer recognizable as a tree.

Right now its soft decay is being exploited by lichens. Patches of parmelia smear it like a gray-green disease. In this rich dead flesh the parmelia grows higher and frillier than it does on the rocks along the shore. But its fanciest frills are nothing in comparison to the ambitious shapes some nearby lichens take. At one spot along the trunk there is an uprising of tiny gray goblet lichens and others with scarlet caps called British soldiers. Still another lichen is usnea moss, or old-man's-beard, whose pale brown wisps are caught like lint on every remaining branch of this spruce corpse. The mosses have mingled with the lichens to produce dazzling little gardens of green, red and gray. Next to the fallen trunk is its moldering stump, with a baby

LIFE CYCLE: A BABY SPRUCE SPRINGING FROM A ROTTED STUMP

spruce—symbol of renewal—growing in its lap.

We stroll on, through an area of mistletoe infestation where dead and dying trees outnumber the healthy ones. Some of them have enormous goiters bulging from their trunks.

"They look terrible," says Packard, "but they don't seem to hurt the trees."

"What are they?"

"Burls. Or, more properly, galls. They're caused by an insect or a fungus that gets under the bark and triggers a tumorlike growth."

A few large rocks begin rearing up along the forest path. Another 50 yards, and they are a dominant part of the landscape. They are pinkish, extremely rough in texture, a mixture of quartz, hornblende, feldspar and mica called pegmatite. This is an igneous rock that resembles a very

coarse granite. It was formed by the cooling of molten material more than 300 million years ago and is about the same age as the banks of finer-grained metamorphic rock on the shore where our walk began. It is astonishing to think that the underpinnings of one little island can have had such different origins.

The path leads down between two bungalow-sized boulders into a narrow black opening that turns out to be a cave with a twisting black passage. We feel our way through, and emerge facing a sheer rock slab 20 feet high with yet another lichen growing on it, large greenish sheets of it with tattered curling edges. This is rock tripe, and is green only at the moist and shady bottom of the slab. Up higher it has been dried and blackened by the sun.

"All these lichens here," muses

Packard. "Do you ever see lichens in New York?"

"No. I can't say that I do."

"There's plenty of good rock for them in all those skyscrapers."

"That's true. Why no lichens on them?"

"Because the air is too bad. Nearly all lichens need clean fresh air, the kind they get right here."

That gives me something to think about. Since lichens were initial fashioners of the land environment on which all green plants now depend, and since all animals depend on green plants—as they do, directly or indirectly—then the lichen bears a large responsibility for man, who is now busily polluting the atmosphere and destroying the very thing that helped make his existence possible. Suddenly those patches of primitive life we have been seeing

RED-CAPPED "BRITISH SOLDIER" LICHENS ON A FALLEN SPRUCE

GRAY GOBLET LICHEN

do not seem as tough and enduring as they did at first.

We scramble up another boulder and find ourselves out of the woods and on the western shore of the island, facing the open sea. There is no beach here, just a jumble of huge pegmatite blocks disappearing in a surf that is gentle today, swirling quietly in the rock clefts. But the vegetation on this shore testifies to an abundance of less benign days.

The things that grow here look durable. They are gnarled and low-lying, clawing their way out of the woods a hard-earned inch at a time, consolidating themselves while they explore soil-filled cracks in the rock that lead still farther out.

Packard explains that this is essentially a more northerly vegetation, either a relic of the colder past, or one that is gradually working its way south, colonizing the harsher corners of the coast. The rank weeds of the island's other side, by contrast, are more southern in origin —although some of them, like cord grass, also grow on the western side.

Sturdy Dwellers on a Rugged Shore

In the edge of the woods is a bed of cinnamon fern, the only fern hardy enough to grow out here. Next to it is some extremely low-growing juniper. It looks like a stunted version of the juniper we encountered earlier near the blackberry bushes. It is *Juniperus horizontalis,* the northern juniper. It, too, is found only on this bleak shore. Still denser and lower, almost like a doormat, is a mass of crowberry, a common plant in Newfoundland and Labrador. The dark

CORD GRASS IN A ROCK CRACK

purplish berry ripens late in the fall, in plenty of time for migrating shore birds—curlews, plovers, godwits —to stoke up on before starting their nonstop flights to the West Indies and South America. This berry was the favorite food of the Eskimo cur-

lew, a bird that formerly gathered on the Northeast coast by the millions, but was so ferociously hunted that no specimen has been seen here for 60 years and the species is believed to be extinct. Mixed in with the crowberry are sprays of another northern variety of plant that has a better-known cousin farther south: mountain cranberry.

Our walk is over. We have come less than half a mile, but have traveled through a wide variety of life zones and 350 million years of geological time. We have stopped to look at only a fraction of the plants that grow on the island. We could come back tomorrow with new eyes for new lichens, new fungi, new ber-

TWO STALWARTS: CINNAMON FERN AND GNARLED SPRUCE

ries, new flowers. We could study the insect life of the island, keep a lookout for other birds that come here, ravens, red-breasted nuthatches, crossbills—all of them species with a northern accent.

As far as animals are concerned, our host shakes his head.

"We have meadow voles and a few small snakes. Sometimes a deer swims over, but that's about it."

There are no raccoons, no skunks, no weasels, no foxes here, no rabbits, squirrels or chipmunks. This explains the great abundance of mushrooms, which elsewhere are nibbled down by chipmunks. There are not even any turtles or frogs in a small marsh near the center of the island. We pass by there late in the day and encounter more plants: jewelweed, skunk cabbage, cattails.

Clearly the lure of this place is its vegetation, the unusually wide spectrum of types found in a small space. I have no idea of the total number of different plant species found on these few fragrant acres, but the figure must be well up in the hundreds. And still we encounter new ones wherever we look. Strolling back to our host's house, we stumble over fresh species. The small meadow in which the house stands contains a new constellation of grasses and summer flowers: timothy, Indian paintbrush, hawkweed. A big clump of roses grows by his doorstep.

"Did you bring these over from the mainland?" I ask.

"No," he replies with a smile. "They grow wild here—just like everything else."

PEGMATITE BLOCKS ON THE ISLAND'S WESTERN SHORE

3/ Between High Tide and Low

Great fleas have little fleas upon their backs to bite 'em,
And little fleas have lesser fleas, and so ad infinitum.

AUGUSTUS DE MORGAN/ *A BUDGET OF PARADOXES*

Rock, sand and tide. One made by convulsions in the earth, another by gravity and time, a third by the moon and sun. These are the ingredients that make up a special world of fantastic intricacy along the Northeast coast, a narrow ribbon of a world, its boundaries marked by the twice-daily slow breath of the ocean as it floods against the land and then back into the deep again.

Just below the lowest fall of the lowest tide is a world that is forever wet, inhabited by things for which the air means death. Just above the highest reach of the highest tide live things that will drown if submerged too long. In between them is a galaxy of plants and animals that have had to adjust themselves to both worlds. For most of them the "real" world is still a wet one. They need water to live, and when the downward suck of the tide leaves them stranded they must wait out their exposure to the air, shut tight, their activity suspended until the water returns again.

The tidal zone of the Northeast coast is one of the most interesting and varied in the world. Two factors help make it so. One is the rockiness and irregularity of the coast. These features of structure create an endless number of coves that empty at low tide, and pools that become isolated cups and bowls brimming with life. The rock itself, being relatively immovable and enduring, is something to which plants and animals can attach themselves. It is full of cracks and small holes in which things can hide. There swarms a richness of life, clinging, waving to and fro, scuttling, shredding, eating and dying—in one miniature natural aquarium after another.

But all is not sheltered coves and pools. Much of the coast is bold headland, exposed to the open sea. Even here plants and animals can establish themselves, gripping the rock and withstanding the smash of the surf. In the midst of the watery tumult minute animals live out their lives, riding the surf gales in the thrashing tops of seaweed trees and hiding among their roots.

On the rocky shore all is in plain view, particularly if the area is one where there is a large rise and fall of tide. This creates the second condition that makes the Northeast coast a special place. A big tide means not only that the opportunities for viewing are good, with various levels exposed at different hours of the day, but also that the zone itself is big. In the tropics, where the tidal rise is often only a foot or two, there is simply not enough space, not enough difference in living conditions between the top of the tidal zone and the bottom, for there to be much difference in the life forms that inhabit its various levels. But where the tidal zone may be 20 to 40 feet in height, as it is sometimes in Maine and the Maritimes, the forms that live near the top of the zone spend most of their time in the air and are entirely different from those that live near the bottom and spend most of their time under water.

Many stretches of rock along the Northeast coast can quite easily be seen to be divided into six separate life zones. I can remember as a youngster clambering around the rocks of a tidal basin in Maine and being vaguely aware of this cluster of environments, but having no sense of its organization, and taking it so for granted that I paid no attention, particularly since the highest zone did not seem to contain life at all. It was a dark band that seemed to stain the rocks just above high tide. I assumed that it was just that—a stain—made by some mysterious interaction of sun and salt, because it was everywhere, always a foot or so above high water, where the flood tide itself never quite reached, but where the rock was intermittently dampened by spray. This ignorance continued until one unforgettable morning when a marine biologist introduced another boy and me to the logic of tidal zones.

That dark stain, he explained, was alive. It consisted of enormous numbers of very small organisms called blue-green algae. These were among the oldest and most primitive of all living things, plantlike organisms related to bacteria. There are more than 2,000 different kinds of blue-green algae around the world, and they are always found in or

Levels of Life on a Rocky Shore

Along the rocks of the Northeast coast, marine life is arranged in strata as rigidly defined as social classes. Only here the distinction is not one of wealth or birth but the ability of the various species to endure exposure to air and to adapt to the demands of dry land.

The strata, called zones, are six in all—starting below the level of low tide and ascending to above the high-water mark. In the lowest zone, continually submerged by the ocean, swarm a host of creatures. In the highest zone, splashed only by sea spray, a few species live a rarefied existence. Between these extremes are the intertidal zones, alternately exposed and submerged during the twice-daily tides. As in most societies, there is a degree of mobility: a creature born into one zone may climb higher or lower in search of more living space or better food.

Whatever zone they occupy, all the marine species must meet the shore's basic challenges. Temperature variations are severe. Ice grinds in winter. Rains wash the salt away. Waves break with relentless violence against the rocks. But there are compensations. Food is plentiful in a well-linked chain. And by adapting to this harsh environment, most coastal species have improved their chances for continued survival.

Seen at low tide, a tidal pool in Maine's Acadia National Park reveals the six zones of plant and animal life found on the rocks of the Northeast coast.

BLACK ZONE

PERIWINKLE ZONE

BARNACLE ZONE

ROCKWEED ZONE

IRISH MOSS ZONE

LAMINARIAN ZONE

The Boundary of Land and Sea: The Black Zone

This zone, an area just below dry land and just above the high-water mark, retains its contact with the sea only through the spray of waves. It has been colonized by some of earth's most ancient plants, the blue-green algae, so minute that from afar they look like a uniform black smudge. Individual plants are clad in gelatinous sheaths that prevent them from drying in the sun and air. Periwinkles from the zone below move up to graze on the algae.

Living at the Evolutionary Limits: The Periwinkle Zone

Only the highest of the monthly tides submerge this zone. Its chief inhabitant, a marine snail called the rough periwinkle, may be on the verge of evolving into a land creature. It can endure extended exposure to air and, like most land snails, produces fully formed young from eggs that hatch inside the mother.

Home of the Tough: The Barnacle Zone

The third zone, exposed to air twice daily for several hours at a time, takes the sea's heaviest pounding. Here barnacles predominate, gluing themselves tightly to rocks and feeding on minute organisms brought in with the tides. Barnacles in turn serve as meals for dog whelks, carnivorous marine snails that force the barnacle shells open and devour the shrimplike contents.

A Gentler Shelter: The Rockweed Zone

This zone, lying below the barnacle zone, is less exposed to air. Stout, rubbery seaweeds called rockweeds, or sea wracks, provide secure shelter for mussels, common periwinkles, smooth periwinkles, crabs and limpets—a species of snail with a flattish, conical shell. The limpet attaches itself to a particular spot on a rock and remains there during low tide; it moves out to feed as the tide comes in and then returns to the same spot, its "home."

A Crowded Place: The Irish Moss Zone

This zone, which is exposed to air only during the lowest of the monthly tides, teems with marine life. Red-brown Irish moss and shiny green sea lettuce mat the rocks and protect the denizens of this zone from the force of waves. Crabs, sea urchins and starfish roam through the moss in a constant search for food.

The Ocean's Threshold: The Laminarian Zone

Conditions in this lowest zone closely approximate those of the ocean, where little sunshine penetrates the deeper waters. In this dark and icy zone, the long, slender laminarias sway to the water's surge. Like rockweeds, laminarias belong to the group of brown algae whose Greek name, Phaeophyceae, means "dusky plants"; they are believed to have originated at a time when the earth lay darkened by a constant cover of heavy clouds. The zone is inhabited by crabs, sea urchins, starfish, anemones, sponges, marine worms and the ancient jellyfish—unchanged in half a billion years.

near water. The particular kind that we were looking at as we squatted on the rocks, the sun hot on the backs of our necks, was very hardy. It protected itself in a gelatinous covering that resisted drying for a long time; a few splashes from the waves would quickly restore it. I reached out a finger to touch this seemingly dead material that my eye had passed over so often but that had never registered on my brain. Slimy, rubbery. Alive! I have since stepped on it more than once when it was wet, and can testify that it is the slipperiest stuff around—climbing over it is a good way to break a leg.

That morning I have never forgotten. I was next introduced to a horde of little snails crammed into a crack in the rock, like commuters on a suburban line huddled together under the station roof on a rainy morning. But these commuters were not huddled out of the rain but out of the sun. They were rough periwinkles, little dark snails with corrugated shells, the largest ones only half an inch long. Down below them in the clear water were other periwinkles of a different kind, slightly larger ones with smoother shells.

"Those ones down in the water," our guide said, "are common periwinkles. They don't come up here quite as much; they can't stand so much fresh air. Farther down, if you look carefully, you'll find still another kind, smooth periwinkles. They never come up here at all. But these fellows"—he picked up a whole handful of the rough periwinkles—"they like it up here. They only need a little water once in a while. As long as the rocks are wet they crawl around and eat the algae growing there. They even go up into the black zone sometimes and eat it."

"How do they eat?" I asked.

"With a radula. That's a kind of tongue coiled like a typewriter ribbon on the underside of the periwinkle near where his mouth is. The ribbon is covered with sharp little spikes or teeth, and he scratches things loose with them. When he wears his teeth down he unrolls a little more of the ribbon so that he can put some fresh teeth to work."

We stared, fascinated, at the rough periwinkles. They were all sizes, down to unbelievably tiny, fragile ones not more than an eighth of an inch long. "Babies?"

"Right, babies."

But these were special babies. They had developed inside their mothers and been born right there on the rocks. The other two kinds of periwinkles deeper down could be born only from eggs laid in the water. But the rough periwinkles were in the process of abandoning the water, following a path taken in the past by all the snails that now live on land. The rough periwinkle has come halfway on that journey. Though it is leaving the water, it still needs a dash of wetness from time to time. Right now—today—it can go up to a month without water. Submerge it too long, and it may drown.

We watched, almost expecting to see one bold periwinkle take off and march up into the forest, but the evolutionary process was too slow; on that particular morning it did not happen. A million years from now, it may have happened.

Now that we were looking at the rough periwinkles in a new way —in a way that encouraged us to understand what periwinkle life was like in terms of periwinkle needs—their distribution on the rocks began to make some sense. Like the black-colored algae just above them, they, too, occupied a zone. Not as obvious a strip as the black zone, since they were able to creep about, but still a strip, crowded with snails in some spots, bare of them in others. Nowhere were they so high as to risk the danger of drying out completely, nowhere so low as to become dangerously submerged for too long. Instead they were always clustered where the living was best for them, on rocks that were damp a good deal of the time but submerged very little of the time.

This insight into periwinkle life made us look at the cove with new and sharper eyes.

"See any other zones?" our guide asked.

We did, instantly. Just below the rough periwinkles was a band of white that jumped out at us—a barnacle zone. Clusters of little tent-shaped white shells crowded here and there, glued to the rocks, but once again in a horizontal band.

While we had been talking and looking, the water had fallen lower and lower in the tidal pool. The fourth zone, the rockweed zone, was now fully exposed. The weed lay everywhere, gleaming piles of rich brown rubbery stuff, its stalks smooth, its "leaves" puffed out into little pea-sized balloons that would buoy the rockweed up again when the tide came in, turning it once more into a dense thicket of small marine trees standing in the water, instead of the inert jumble that now lay piled on the ledges or dangled helplessly from the rocks. Like everything else in the tidal zone, the rockweed has its limits. It is more tolerant of changing conditions than some of the other organisms, and thus can inhabit a wider band than they. But it needs at least an hour of submergence on every tide; this marks the upper level at which it can grow. Farther down, it runs into competition from other kinds of sea-

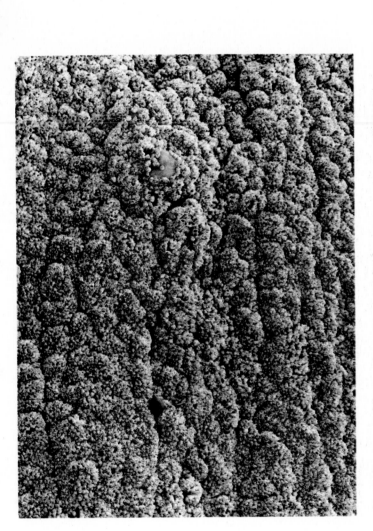

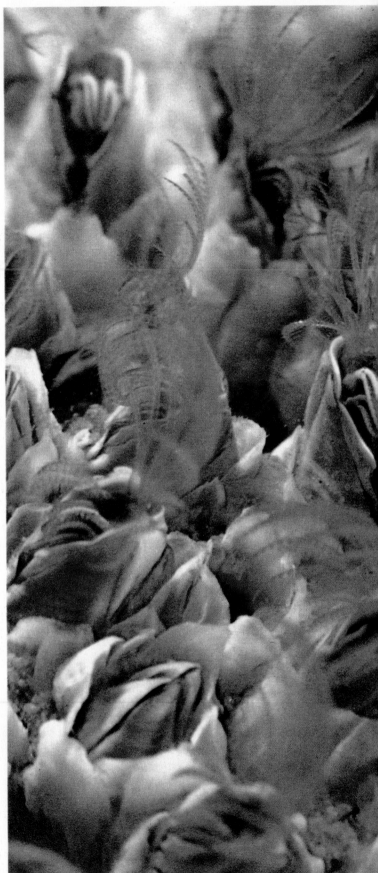

A colony of acorn barnacles (above) occupies every inch of available rock between high- and low-tide levels at Louds Island, Maine. The larvae of these crustaceans use a powerful glue to cement themselves safely to the wave-pounded rock. Here the barnacle builds itself a conical shell and lives for about five years. Motionless at low tide, it springs into action the moment water covers it (right), waving six pairs of feathery legs. Three pairs filter food particles from the water while the other three scrape off the food and deposit it in the creature's mouth.

weed that are better adapted to extract food-making sunlight from deeper dimmer water. But in between, rockweed is the dominant plant. It grows so luxuriantly that it becomes a haven for a great number of small animals as they wait out the return of the tide, hiding from the sun in its safe soggy layers and venturing out to conduct their business among the standing fronds only after the waters have come back.

Turn over a heap of rockweed that has been lying in the sun for a few hours and has become so dried out that its shiny surface looks dull —a dusty yellow brown turning almost black. Kick that scuffed, leathery top layer aside. An inch down, there will be a huddle of minute squirmers and crawlers—tiny crabs, worms, snails.

Just below the rockweed is a fifth level of tidal life, the Irish moss zone. Irish moss is squatter, denser and redder than rockweed. Where it is well established the rockweed cannot get a foothold. The two meet in rubbery confrontation near the bottom of the tidal zone, so deep down that only on flood tides, when the pull of sun and moon are lined up and the rise and fall of water is greater than usual, is the Irish moss exposed to air.

Like all plants, Irish moss needs light. It crowds as high as it can, leaving the deeper darker waters to another group of plants that occupy the sixth and lowest tidal zone. These are laminarias; a commoner name for them is kelp. Laminarias generally shun the air and are seldom found growing within exposed parts of the tidal zone, although they must be considered a part of it since the tops of individual plants penetrate it regularly, rising and falling with the tide. Laminarias anchor themselves to the bottom, sometimes in very deep water, and send up long brown beltlike ribbons in search of the sun. In the giant kelp beds of the Pacific coast these ribbons sometimes reach lengths of 150 feet. Here in the Northeast a 20-foot ribbon is a big one. The most common local laminaria is a variety called horsetail kelp. It has a short, strong single stalk from the top of which bursts a cluster of a dozen or so straplike strands. At very low water the strands float on the surface like pieces of harness.

Standing on a rocky point on a still summer day, with the sea like glass except for the slow heaves and sighs that characterize it as a presence that is never truly still, one can scarcely imagine the fury of the storms that on other days or in other seasons possess it. Scientists have calculated that the pressure exerted by big waves sometimes runs as high as 1½ tons per square foot of rock surface. How any plant or animal can endure that crushing force is hard to understand, particularly when one considers how delicately made some of them are. The acorn barnacle, that champion colonizer of exposed intertidal rock, survives by erecting a hard tepee-shaped house of six little slabs that come together but do not quite meet in the center. The barnacle lies snug inside, impervious to the crash of the waves, and makes its living through the hole in its tepee roof, sweeping in food with its legs. The hole is fitted with a four-piece trap door, which closes for protection against the air when the tide is out. Once the barnacle is firmly glued to the rock, it could not care less about surf. The wonder is that it chooses such an apparently inhospitable place to live.

Its hazardous homesite is only one of the fascinations of this extraordinary little animal. Entire books have been written about barnacles. Charles Darwin spent much of his life studying them. They can in fact stand as an example of all life in the tidal pool. Every animal there has its own little astonishment, if we could only linger long enough to learn it, enlarge our eyes sufficiently to see it. Therefore, it seems to me, something of the complexity of one life should be touched on if one is to grasp the complexity that is everywhere here.

Barnacles are not what they seem. Since they sit in one place inside a "shell," one might assume that they are something like clams, mussels and snails—that group of hard-shelled, soft-bodied sea creatures called mollusks. But barnacles are not mollusks. They are arthropods, as different from clams as they are from camels.

Arthropods probably comprise the largest broad grouping of animals on earth. Each member of the phylum—and there are nearly a million of them—has an exoskeleton (i.e., the "bones" that hold it together are on the outside of its body in the form of a thin but hard covering like that worn by a lobster, rather than on the inside, as in human beings). An arthropod also has stiff shell-encased legs (again like a lobster's), with several joints each. All insects are arthropods, as are mites, spiders, centipedes and an important marine group known as crustaceans. The crustaceans include lobsters, crabs, shrimp—and barnacles. Pry open the hard white tepee of a barnacle, and inside will be found a 12-legged creature that looks like a very small shrimp. It will not try to dart off when its home is broken open; it cannot. The first thing a barnacle does when settling down is to cement the back of its head to the rock. This done, it can never move again. It builds a limestone fort around itself and spends the rest of its life lying on its back—as one scientist has put it—kicking food into its mouth with its feet.

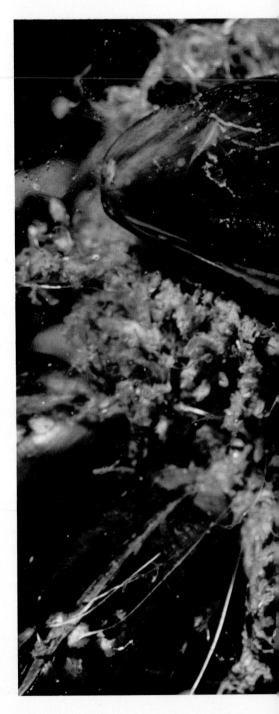

An acorn barnacle, like all crustaceans, starts life as a tiny larva called a nauplius. It is expelled into the sea at birth along with millions of brother-sisters (sex in a barnacle is not simple), and spends the next few months floating aimlessly about in the water, swimming feebly with feathery little appendages. Although at this stage it bears no resemblance whatsoever to the animal it will become, it already betrays its crustacean heritage by having an exoskeleton that it has to shed periodically as it grows. During one of these molts it changes form entirely, and for a short while it lives through the second stage of typical crustacean development as a cypris. This creature is so different from the nauplius that if observations had not confirmed that one springs from the other, their relationship could not be imagined. Outside, the cypris has a vague resemblance to a very small semitransparent clam. Inside, it is entirely different, a complex little animal with six pairs of legs, a central nervous system and the rudiments of an eye (which will disappear again in the adult form, since mature barnacles have no need for vision).

As it grows, the cypris gradually seeks out deeper and deeper levels in the water. Finally, responding to some kind of triggering device that is not well understood, it drops to the bottom and begins to creep about on the rock, looking for a place to settle.

If that were all there was to it, there would be little mystery. But there would also be acorn barnacles scattered everywhere, instead of huge colonies of them clustered in the narrow zone they occupy near the high-water mark. Why do the frail little cyprides go up there to be dashed about by the waves, to be swept away again and again? How are they given time to explore the rocks for acceptable resting places? How do they catch hold? Strangest of all, why do they select areas that are out of the water much of the time when they are themselves animals that can feed only under the water?

There are no sure answers to these questions, only logical ones, of which three suggest themselves as probable. First, the deeper-water surfaces to which a cypris might attach itself are often so slimed by other growths that it cannot find a suitable home there, and must keep looking until by design or chance it finds itself in the upper, more dangerous levels of the surf where the rock is cleaner. Second, those that do find suitable living places deep in the water are probably eaten fairly promptly by predatory snails, and thus do not survive long enough to form significant colonies. Finally, there seems to be an attraction of bar-

nacle for barnacle. Is this a chemical "scent" released in the water by existing colonies, to which the searching cyprides respond? Again, nobody is certain. All that is clear is that barnacles crowd in great numbers in the so-called barnacle zone, and that they find their way there somehow after months of aimless drifting elsewhere. A cypris could conceivably anchor down a hundred miles from where it was born.

In the critical hours after the moment of attachment, how does the cypris become a barnacle? There seems to be no answer. The creature grabs hold, and in a few moments is cemented in place. Instantly a miracle starts working. Within a day it transforms itself a second time. Its cypris form is replaced by the shrimplike body of an adult barnacle. At the same time the six plates of its protective house are formed, also out of the tissue of the cypris, together with the four-piece trap door.

As soon as its transformation is complete, the barnacle begins the activity that will occupy it without letup for the rest of its life. When the tide is in and the water swarming with minute particles of living food, it opens its trap door, sticks out its legs, which have delicate feathery fronds on them, waves them about momentarily as a fisherman would a small net, then draws them in again with a tiny haul of nourishment, and eats what it has caught. Every few seconds it goes through this action, and two boys crouching in the shallows of a tidal pool a good many years ago were taught how to look for the movements of the barnacle colony as the tide comes in. One by one, as the water covers them, the barnacles will come to life with a quick flicker of legs here, another flicker there. Soon the entire colony will be waving and feeding.

With all that eating, a barnacle is bound to grow. As it did in the nauplius and cypris stages, the adult barnacle must shed its exoskeleton from time to time. This it does periodically for the three to five years of normal barnacle life. However, it soon finds its house too small. To solve this problem, the barnacle secretes a chemical that dissolves the inner surface of the house to make more room inside, while at the same time adding to the outer surface. It is as if a man living in a concrete igloo were to spend his time chipping material from his interior walls and plastering it back on the outside. Gradually his igloo would get bigger and bigger, but the walls would get increasingly thin. The barnacle gets the extra plaster to keep the walls of its house thick from other chemicals it secretes for this purpose. When their owners die, the houses stand empty on the rocks. Other small animals then use them as hiding places, or other young barnacles settle down in them.

Perched on a sprig of rockweed, a smooth periwinkle crouches beneath its polished shell. Unlike its cousins, the common periwinkle and the rough periwinkle—both able to survive out of water—this marine snail is tied to the sea, for it can endure only the briefest exposure to air. Moreover, the smooth periwinkle can live only amid the colonies of rockweed below the high-tide level, since it feeds on tiny organisms that cling to these algae.

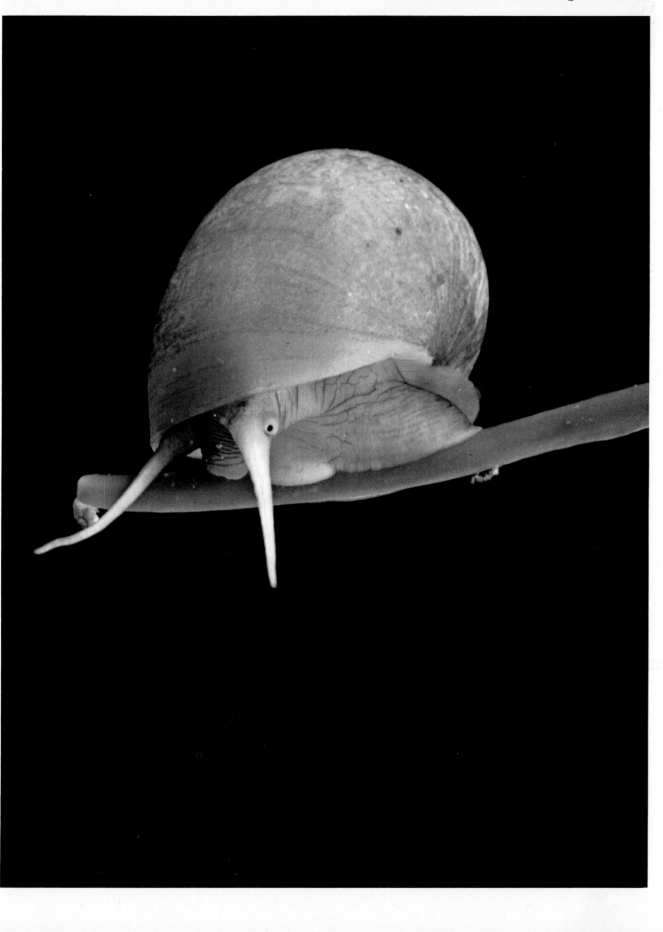

As every boatowner knows, barnacles will also attach themselves to boat bottoms. The "nonfouling" paint used to prevent barnacle encrustation contains minute grains of poison that are exposed little by little as the paint leaches away during the course of a summer. But sooner or later the poison action will cease and the bottom of the boat will become slimy, a veritable zoo of algae and tiny worms, with barnacles rearing up like snowy mountain peaks over this minute marine jungle. From the point of view of a barnacle there could be no better home than a boat bottom. A barnacle's worst enemies are carnivorous snails, along with starfish and certain marine worms. Inasmuch as all these creatures creep along the sea bottom in search of their prey, there is no way they can get at something floating overhead. A boat bottom is such a safe place for barnacles that a hull not attended to regularly will become covered with the creatures. Over the years I have scraped away thousands of them with a putty knife.

The barnacle's method of establishing a home and making a living, complex as it seems, is simple compared to its sex life. Most barnacles are hermaphroditic—each individual has both male and female sex organs. The eggs that are produced by the female part of the individual are not fertilized by its own male organ but by the organ of a neighbor, which can stretch out for several inches to fertilize any barnacle within reach. Thus it is possible for barnacle A to mate with barnacle B in two ways simultaneously. Or, barnacle B can mate with barnacle A in one way, while it is mating with barnacle C in another.

This free-wheeling sexual activity is all very well for acorn barnacles, which live in dense colonies with potential sexual partners close at hand. But what about some of the kinds that lead entirely different lives? There is one species, for example, that attaches itself to a certain shrimp. Since the shrimp cannot ordinarily support more than one barnacle there is no chance for such a barnacle to find a sexual partner. It solves the problem by eliminating males entirely. Only females are produced—from eggs that develop without fertilization.

Forgetting barnacles for a moment, I turn away and peer deeper into the water, feeling myself drawn down—down among the waving fronds, into a world whose private rules, manners and relationships grow more intricate as one descends. There are more—and odder —creatures down here.

In the middle of the rockweed zone, which is under water fully half the time, the plants stand like a protective forest. Roving its glades, lurk-

With its graceful languor masking an insatiable appetite, a sea anemone stretches its tentacles in search of prey. The instant an unwary passerby brushes against a tentacle, thousands of cells shoot forth microscopic spears containing a paralyzing poison. The sea anemone then brings the victim to its mouth at the center of its body and devours the catch. Totally indiscriminate in its choice of food, this glutton even tries eating fellow anemones—but finds them indigestible.

ing in its thickets, are its most conspicuous denizens, the mollusks —various kinds of snails, clams and, most conspicuous of all, great beds of mussels. Gastronomically the mussel of the Northeastern coast is a most underrated animal, which is a lucky thing for the visitor who likes to eat them. I know of few pleasanter diversions during a coastal cruise than to row ashore at half tide in a cove where large mussels abound, collect a bucket of them, and then spend the rest of the afternoon lazily cleaning them. You sit in the sun on the deckhouse of your boat with the bucket between your legs, watching the forested islets slide by as you sail toward the harbor where you will anchor for the night. Idly you take a mussel from the bucket, rub the slime off it with your thumb, pick away the threadlike beard that grows on it, and then drop it into another bucket of fresh sea water. There it will purge itself, getting rid of bits of sand and mud, completing its digestive activities. By the time you have reached your harbor the sun will be low, the air will be cool and bracing, the mussels will be clean, and you will have a ferocious appetite.

Steam the mussels in a large covered pot in half an inch of sea water, adding a touch of garlic and a little white wine. There is nothing to match the delicious gush of salty, mussely, steamy aroma that suffuses the cabin of your boat when the mussels are dumped out of the pot, their shells open and gleaming, their flesh a rich salmon color—except, of course, the eating of them. Be sure you have plenty of melted butter. You can down two dozen of them without even blinking.

A mussel—like a clam or a scallop—is a bivalve, an animal with two shells that cover it top and bottom and are hinged at the back. To protect itself against enemies or against drying out, the bivalve can close its shells tightly together, the two halves fitting so neatly that no air can get in. Closure is made perfect by a soft growing layer around the edge of the shell, a seal as efficient as the gasket in an automobile engine. A mussel regularly closes itself against the outside world for anywhere from one to six hours on each complete tidal cycle. When the water returns, it opens again.

Unlike clams and other bivalves that bury themselves in sand or mud and do their breathing and feeding through long necks that they poke up to clear water, mussels live out their lives in plain view. Like barnacles, they apparently have some chemical attraction for one another, since they crowd together in dense colonies. A flourishing mussel bed in a tidal cove is something to see. The handsome black shells, shot with steely blue, are jammed so closely—packed solid on the rocks, clinging in clusters to the stems and holdfasts of every weed, piled on each other, little ones wedged between big ones—that there seems to be no possibility that one more mussel of whatever size could fit in.

It is this problem of living space, far more than that of feeding, that is the principal concern of many fixed, or "sessile," animals living along the shore. For food there is the literally endless abundance of the tiny organisms of the sea. All that is needed is sufficient movement of the water to bring this food to the animal: current, tide, surf. This movement is intensified by the actions of the creature itself, which creates a small local current by the agitation of feelers, by the waving of hairs or legs, or by suction. So rich is the marine food supply that every last mussel in a mussel bed, no matter how densely populated, probably gets all the food it needs.

Should a young mussel find a suitable spot, it will anchor itself by producing a thin thread of elastic material, called a byssus, which hardens on contact with salt water. As it excretes one of these byssus threads, the mussel quickly fastens the end to the rock, then it produces another, and another, spreading them around like miniature guy wires until it is firmly rooted in place by a healthy bunch of strands.

To fasten down—and to grow. The chances that a young mussel will live to maturity are fantastically slim. In the sea, being small is a terrible hazard, you may be eaten by anything larger, including your own parents. A clam that is industriously sucking food particles down through its siphon cannot distinguish between clam larvae and other tiny organisms; it may end up eating thousands of its own offspring, having given birth to them only a few days before.

To combat the undiscriminating toll that is taken of their eggs and larvae, mollusks reproduce on a prodigious scale. A healthy female mussel can produce more than 20 million eggs at one spawning. The presence of the eggs triggers the release of a larger ejaculation of sperm cells from nearby male mussels. The eggs are fertilized in the water, and quickly go through several stages of development as free-swimming little creatures before they turn into recognizable mussels and try to find a place to settle. Each day that an infant mussel lives it grows a little larger, and gradually escapes from one class after another of predators for which it has become too big to be devoured. Even so, the carnage goes on, from snails, crabs, starfish, worms, birds.

Among the principal and most relentless predators of the tidal pool are poky, seemingly harmless snails. The most conspicuous of these is

Moon jellies, a type of common
jellyfish, lie attached to the underside
of a rock in one stage of a process
called strobilization. Resembling
primitive plants, the long stalks, or
strobilae, are made up of connected
rings, each destined to be a young
moon jelly. As the outer end segments
—fully formed and furnished with
petallike tentacles for gathering food
—detach themselves, each of the disks
farther up the stalks is growing,
flattening and preparing in its turn to
assume the starlike shape of a jellyfish.
The free-floating moon jellies, called
medusae (after the terrifying woman of
Greek myth who had writhing snakes
for hair), are most often seen washed
up on beaches or lurking, milkily
translucent, in the waters offshore.

the dog whelk. It is about the size of a common periwinkle, but is more pointed at its tip and is often striped in handsome alternate bands of brown and white. Reach into a pool and pick up a periwinkle and a dog whelk. Each will withdraw into its shell and lie motionless in your hand. At first glance, the two will seem so alike in form and function that it is almost impossible to realize how different they are. One is the cow of the tidal pool, the other the wolf. One uses its radula to scrape algae from the rocks, the other to bore holes in mussel shells and get at the living tissue inside. The mussels have absolutely no defense against such attack. Unable to move, they lie where they are, slowly being eaten alive. Barnacles are disposed of with equal ease; the whelk simply forces its foot inside the trap door in the barnacle's roof, holding the door open while it dines on the occupant.

Lower down in the pool lurk other killers: crabs with powerful pincers for crushing tender young shells, anemones and jellyfish offering a paralyzing embrace for anything that blunders their way.

Anemones squat on the rock and, when open, look like flowers—magnificent blossoms in brilliant shades of green, red and orange. Their chrysanthemumlike "petals" are their tentacles, springing up around a central mouth. Some anemones have more than a thousand such tentacles, each capable of separate movement, each armed with sharp, poisonous little darts coiled inside sacs. Let any small creature touch the tentacle, and several darts will automatically be fired, spearing and paralyzing the unfortunate animal that triggers them. This food is then conveyed by the tentacle to the central mouth, pushed in and digested. The same mouth is also used for defecation, since the body of the anemone is shaped like a test tube, with only one opening at the top, an attribute that identifies it as a coelenterate, along with jellyfish, hydroids and corals. The bottom end of the anemone is covered by a thick pad for holding on to the rock.

Anemones are adaptable animals. If they are disturbed, they quickly retract all their tentacles, so that what was a gorgeous flower an instant ago is now a small, tough, rubbery brown lump somewhat the shape of a gumdrop. They also adjust to fluctuations in the food supply. In a rich environment they will grow rapidly. If the food supply is inadequate they simply shrink.

Jellyfish, frail beyond imagining when compared to their tough anemone cousins, enter the tidal pool only by accident. They prefer to lie offshore, since their soft bodies are no match for the pounding of the surf.

Moving through a havoc of mussel shells they have just emptied (above), two starfish continue on the prowl. A closeup view of a starfish skin (right) shows that it is more than a mere covering for this formidable predator. The orange protuberances function like lungs, taking oxygen from the water and releasing carbon dioxide through minute holes. The pink clusters are miniature cleaning mechanisms: fitted with tiny pincers, they keep the "skin lungs" of the starfish from getting clogged by particles of matter that constantly swirl through a tidal pool.

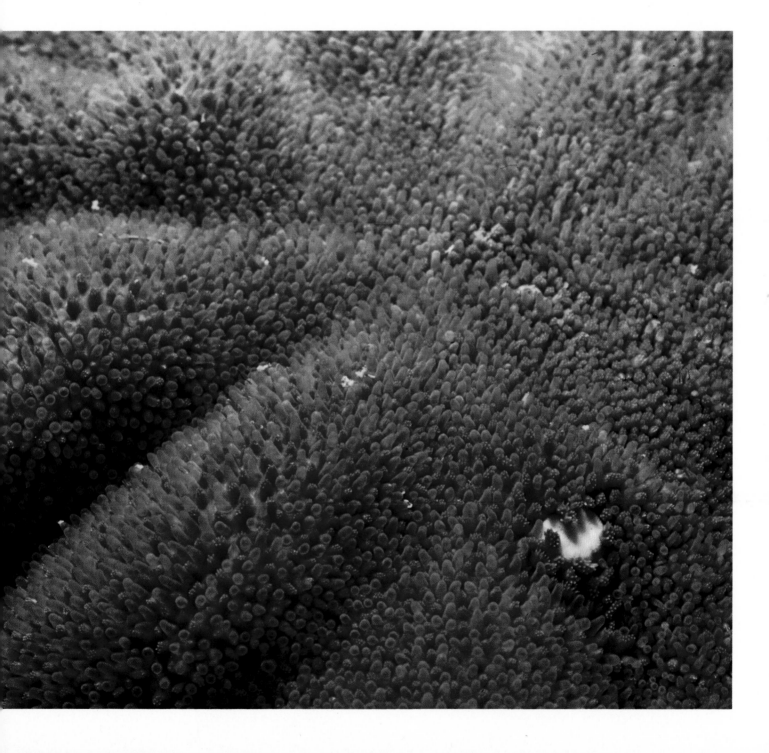

There they flap slowly through the water, trailing their tentacles behind their nearly transparent, bell-shaped bodies. The commonest of the local jellyfish are moon jellies, which grow to a width of about six inches. Their stings are so gentle that they can be handled with little danger. The likelihood of an encounter with one increases with the waning of the summer. Earlier, the moon jellies manage to stay offshore, but toward the end of August they become enfeebled and begin to drift in, sometimes in fantastic numbers. Low tide in a quiet cove will find them stranded by the thousands, one helpless little mound of drying Jell-O after another.

It is during this time that their life cycle is renewed. The larvae, which have been developing under the protecting flaps of their bodies, are now released. At first the little creatures swim about in the tidal pools, subject to all the hazards therein, but eventually they anchor themselves to the bottom and go through a curious plantlike phase that is common to many coelenterates. The anchored larva grows into a kind of stem with tentacles at the top. Thus it spends the winter, its stem becoming ringed with creases that get deeper and deeper as spring approaches. Finally the topmost crease becomes so deep that the tip of the stem breaks off and floats away—a star-shaped creature only a half an inch in diameter, but still a complete moon jelly. It is followed by another small bit of stem, and another, until the stem is exhausted. This process is known as budding.

Starfish belong to yet another marine phylum, the echinoderms. Also in the group are sea urchins, sea cucumbers and some things that look like agile, skinny starfish, the brittle stars. All are found in tidal waters, and all are built to the same basic five-sided or star-shaped body pattern. This structure is not so obvious in the sea urchins and sea cucumbers. The former look like round pincushions with innumerable needlelike spikes sticking out of them. But if the spikes are removed and the hard shell of the pincushion examined carefully, it will be seen to consist of five sections. Similarly, a sea cucumber, while shaped more like a loaf of bread than a starfish, is actually a five-piece animal too—it is just stretched out somewhat.

Starfish are among the most durable creatures of the sea, and among the most interesting. Everything they do they seem to do a little differently from other animals. They have thick, tough skins that actually consist of great numbers of horny plates distributed loosely enough so that their arms can be moved. These plates are covered with bumps or short spikes, giving the surface of the starfish a very rough texture. Most species—including the northern starfish, the common type on the Northeast coast—have five arms. There is no front or rear, and thus no problem of backing up or turning around, which might otherwise be awkward for an animal that is intrinsically rather stiff, slow-moving and clumsy. Sensory organs at the tips of the arms alert the starfish to either food or danger, and it is the direction from which such a stimulus is coming that determines which part of the starfish will momentarily become its "head." The arm nearest the food begins to move toward it, and the rest of the animal cooperates by going along.

Starfish travel in a way peculiar to echinoderms: by the use of tube feet. These are small organs that lie in thick rows on the underside of the starfish. Each has a suction pad on its end. When the starfish wishes to move, it elongates some of these tube feet, fastens them down, and then contracts them again, thus hauling itself ahead a tiny distance. The suction pads are extremely efficient; when a large number of them are used to hold the animal in place, even a heavy wave will not dislodge it. If you try to pick one up from a rock, you will find that it takes a sharp pull to get it loose. When you do get it free, you will probably tear away a good many of its tube feet, which will remain clinging to the rock.

The way starfish breathe is extraordinary. They have innumerable tiny holes in their outer skins, through each of which protrudes a bulge of very thin internal membrane. Each of these minute balloons serves the same function as a lung. On the outside it has hairlike cilia that beat fresh water up against the membrane, which extracts oxygen, just as the membrane in a human lung extracts oxygen from air. The oxygen is then circulated through the body fluid of the starfish by another set of hairs on the inside of the membrane.

Breathing as it does, through organs distributed all over its body, the starfish obviously must keep itself clean. Unlike almost everything else in the tidal pool, where surfaces quickly become coated with a slime of minute animal and vegetable matter, a starfish always looks as fresh as if it had just been scrubbed. It manages this cleanliness with another set of organs that are sprinkled by the thousands all over the upper surface of its body. These are pedicellariae, separate little tweezers that attempt to grab and crush anything that tries to settle on the starfish's back. The pedicellariae are too small to be seen with the naked eye, but their existence can be verified by letting a starfish lie upside down on the back of your hand. In a few moments hundreds of these tweezers

A sea urchin, close relative to the starfish, rests on an underwater rock (above), secure in its hard, prickly shell. Covering the shell are organs that allow the urchin to move, feed and avoid being fed on. As feet, it uses supple suction tubes, which adhere to surfaces by pumping out water and creating a vacuum. It wards off predators by means of sharp spines attached to the shell by ball-and-socket joints; the spines pivot to form an impenetrable barrier against an enemy.

Common as far north as central Maine, the green crab is small but mean. Young clams are its dish, but when confronted with a human being, the two-inch creature will snap its claws so ferociously that the French dubbed it the crabe enragé, or mad crab.

will have seized the hairs on your hand. But their grip is so feeble that you will only just feel it as you remove the starfish.

A starfish's mouth is on its bottom, its anus on top. In feeding, it will slowly prowl over a mussel bed, select a victim, and then get a good hold with a number of its tube feet all along both edges of the mussel's shell. The mussel, of course, clamps itself shut at the first hint that the starfish is there. This does not deter the starfish at all. It is strong and patient. It sets more and more of its tube feet against the two sides of the mussel's shell, and exerts a little more pressure. Slowly, if the starfish has not picked too large and muscular an adversary, the mussel will weaken. It begins to gape open a crack. That is all the starfish needs. It has a very elastic stomach that it sticks out of its own body and inside the shell of the mussel. There it surrounds the soft tissue of the mussel and digests it at its leisure.

Starfish can create such havoc among bivalves, particularly in oyster beds, that commercial fishermen regard them as dreadful menaces. For years, in different parts of the country, fishermen conducted campaigns to eliminate starfish by chopping in two any that they found. This practice has been abandoned as the fishermen have learned that it merely leaves two starfish where there was one before. These animals have remarkable powers of regeneration. Slice off an arm, and another will quickly grow in its place; or perhaps two—it is not all that unusual to find a six-armed or even a seven-armed individual.

There is a starfish below me in the pool as I sit on a rock on Grand Manan Island, New Brunswick. This pool is at the mouth of the Bay of Fundy, and when the tide falls it drops 30 feet. There are pools all along here in the rocks, at different levels like locks in a canal. I don't know if I have picked a good pool or not. All I see at the moment are some bits of seaweed and this one starfish. It is just sitting there, doing nothing. But I settle down to watch, fascinated as always by the promise that each of these crystalline little worlds holds. In a minute I will catch a quick movement: a tumbling snail, the twitch of a marine worm. Once again I will feel myself being drawn down into the water, seeing in my mind's eye the jiggling, throbbing multitude of living specks that I know are there but that are below the threshold of visibility.

I come from this watery world. My ancestors once lived here, once dined on those specks somewhere in the tidal boundaries of a vanished ocean. Somewhere they crawled ashore, bringing with them the mark of their kind. They were vertebrates, and so am I, each of us distin-

guished by having a backbone. So equipped, we have conquered the great world of the air, and I am struck, as I look back into the small pool of water from which we all came, that I can see no vertebrates here now. Every other conceivable device for holding together a living organism seems to be here, but where is something with a backbone? I look again, and I notice a round black dot suspended in the water. It is ringed. It looks like a very small eye. It is an eye—attached to a fish.

It is clear why I have not noticed it before. It is lying motionless in the water. Its body must be made of glass; it is transparent, virtually invisible. I bend over to get a better look. My shadow alarms it and it darts away. Darting with it are four others that I would never have seen if they had not moved. They come to rest again three feet away, once again motionless. I study them, and can make out through those transparent bodies the threadlike shadows of five backbones that connect five sets of eyes to five see-through tails. I don't know what kind of fish these are. They are obviously very young, fragile beyond belief, prisoners for the moment in this cup of sea water, having wandered here on the tide, waiting to go somewhere else when it floods again. I am glad to see them here. They help establish my own connection with the tidal pool, which I can make intellectually, but which I do not truly feel until I see a vertebrate brother down there in the water. All life is related, I know. But who could feel a sense of kinship with a clam?

A sudden shadow brushes the pool—a herring gull overhead—and the wary little fish jink again. I am reminded that while all seems quiet and secure here at the moment, it really isn't. Right now there are probably young crabs backed into crannies, watching those fish, spinning whatever dreams crabs dream, waiting for night to fall so that they can venture safely out. Perhaps only three of the five glass fish will be leaving the pool on the next tide. No matter—there are millions like them, eating and being eaten. Their kind will survive through sheer numbers.

Nothing in the tidal pool is inviolate, nothing really dominant. The living is rich, the opportunities for life almost endless, the carnage enormous. Only a handful of any type manages to live out its allotted span. And yet some always do. Balances are delicate, relationships intricate in the extreme. Every conceivable niche is filled by some life form or another. Each animal or plant in the tidal zone gives its own small twist to the environment, providing a set of living conditions that still another form may be able to adapt itself to. Nature is more fertile in working out these adjustments than the human imagination.

Of what use, for example, are the innumerable periwinkle shells that settle on the bottom of the pool? Their owners are dead, deftly picked out and eaten by predators. But the shells endure, and one animal has learned to make use of them: the hermit crab, so deformed by its specialization that it resembles no other crab in the world. Instead of being boxlike and thick-shelled like most other crabs, it has a soft, vulnerable body that tapers to a point so that it will fit backward into the curling chamber of the periwinkle shell. To protect itself in front, the crab has one outsize pincer that not only helps it snatch food but also serves as a kind of portcullis to barricade the entrance of the shell when it has backed itself in. Never was there so lopsided and peculiar a little crab. How it got that way, how it has learned to hunt about for another larger snail shell when it outgrows the one it is occupying—these questions focus on only one quirk in the thousands of specializations that make life in the tidal pool so endlessly surprising. And if the life of the hermit crab seems specialized, consider that of a worm that lives behind the crab, tucked back up the spiral in the inmost tip of the periwinkle shell. It did not live there when the periwinkle did. It moved in with the crab, and will move again when the crab moves. It lives nowhere else, apparently does the crab no harm, and is never seen except to poke out timidly to nibble up a few crumbs that fall as the crab eats.

Does the worm provide a niche for something still smaller, still more specialized? Perhaps. Maybe someone who reads this book will investigate the matter and discover a still smaller creature living in that even narrower niche, back in the dark, on that odd little worm. But if he does, he will only be posing another question: what lives on *it*?

4/ Riches of the Continental Shelf

*Out of the mystery, shadows, fishing-boats, trailing each
other/Following the cliff for guidance,/Holding a
difficult path between the peril of the sea-fog/And the foam
on the shore granite.*   ROBINSON JEFFERS/ BOATS IN A FOG

Below the tidal zone is another well-marked area of the ocean known as the continental shelf. This is a long, gentle underwater slope on which is deposited the outwash of mud, sand and other stony debris that is carried seaward from the continent. In most places, the shelf runs gradually outward and downward to a depth of about 600 feet before plunging off into the abyss of the true ocean.

As in the tidal zone, conditions for an abundant marine life on the Northeastern continental shelf are superb, mainly because of the cold, rich Labrador Current flowing down from the north. How the current works and why it is so rich are worth examining.

The process that produces the current actually begins in the tropics. The sea water there, heated by the sun, expands, causing the surface level of the ocean to rise slightly at the equator. This in turn produces a slope that, while exceedingly small, is still sufficient to make the equatorial water run "downhill" toward both poles. On its journey a high concentration of oxygen is mixed into it at the surface. As it travels it also cools off, which increases its capacity to hold oxygen—and carbon dioxide as well. By the time this rich mixture reaches extreme northern latitudes, it has become very cold and, as a result of contraction, very heavy. It descends to the bottom of the ocean and flows south again.

Mixed into this frigid, oxygen-rich water from the Arctic, streaming steadily down between Labrador and Greenland, is a good supply of silica, ground out of the quartzes and granites of the northern continent and carried into the sea by rivers and glaciers. The combination of silica and oxygen creates a perfect environment for diatoms, the minute plants that form the base of the oceanic food chain. Diatoms need silica to construct both the boxlike frames that hold them together and the bewildering array of fragile glasslike arms or spines that so many of them have to give them buoyancy in the water.

Being plants, diatoms also need sunlight and carbon dioxide for photosynthesis. The former they find in great abundance in northern latitudes in summer because the days are so long. Consequently—and particularly near the coast, where the concentration of silica is higher than in mid-Atlantic and where the waters are relatively shallow—the bloom of diatoms is almost beyond belief. In bright summer weather they can double their numbers in as little as 24 hours. It is this immense outpouring of food that supports the vast shoals of shrimp, herring and other small fish, and, in turn, the larger fish that have been vital to man's welfare for many thousands of years.

Most of the large fish of the north are wanderers, migrants that travel in great herds from one season to the next, following the currents, sensitive to variations in temperature, in salinity, in the food supply, and obedient to their own spawning instincts, which drive many of them for hundreds or thousands of miles when the urge is on them. Some, like giant tuna, each weighing a quarter of a ton or more, plow their way majestically south in late autumn like squadrons of steely submarines, coming back in June to gorge on smaller fish—haddock, sea bass, cod, salmon—that are also roving the northern seas. The bottom of the continental shelf is equally rich in marine life. It is carpeted with marine worms, mollusks, spider crabs and lobsters.

Unlike the shallower shore-hugging world of the tidal pool, this deeper offshore world cannot be examined at leisure, in detail through a magnifying glass, as it were. It is large, formidable and—to the casual observer—apparently uninhabited. The massed life beneath its surface is betrayed only occasionally by the screaming activity of sea birds, diving on small fish that have been driven dangerously close to the surface by a rush of larger fish from below.

Only once have I encountered a really large fish swimming free in open water. This was in Penobscot Bay in Maine, which I was crossing early one morning under power. No breeze had come up yet and the sea was like glass, enabling me to spot, almost a half mile away, something lazily moving in the water. I first took it to be the dorsal fin of a swordfish, since I knew that swordfish like to lie in warm layers near the surface with their fins protruding. Coming nearer, I turned my engine off and asked my wife to steer right for this fin. I stood in the bowsprit with a long boathook, and as we coasted slowly and silently up over this creature, I could look directly down on it. It was a shark, about 10 feet long, dozing in the water, giving its tail a slow twitch every minute or so just to remind itself that it was a shark. I have never seen anything that looked quite so big. As we came up over it I gave it a poke with the boathook. With a tremendous thrash of its tail it swirled down and out of sight, only to come up again a few hundred yards away and resume its siesta. Again we approached, again a poke and a furious dive—and another surfacing. Apparently this fish was determined to have its rest; we abandoned it.

Apart from a rare encounter like this, one does not come in contact with the large fish of the sea, and there is a sense of deep frustration in surveying the seemingly empty ocean and pondering how to reach and become acquainted with its denizens. The best way to bridge this gulf is by observing or associating with fishermen. They, by extension —through their lines and nets—get down into the waters. They come into contact with fish, with huge numbers of them. They know their ways and their whereabouts.

I first looked a live codfish in the eye 40 years ago. This was in the Gulf of St. Lawrence, where I was sailing with three friends in a small ketch, on our way to the Gaspé and Nova Scotia. I don't remember exactly where it was that we began seeing the fishing boats. We sailed by the first one, a heavy dory anchored half a mile offshore, and watched a man and a boy working with hand lines. Each was tending several lines. As fast as he got one up and unhooked a fish he would begin hauling on the next. While we had them in view they must have caught 10 fish—cod, fat and handsome. Now we were in the thick of the fishing: dories all around us, hands whirling like spinning reels, fish flashing bright arcs in the sun as they were yanked into the boats.

The bait? None, apparently. A man would rip a fish from the hook and throw over his line again without rebaiting it. All it had on the end was a minnow-shaped lead sinker armed with two or three hooks. Were the fish biting at *this*? Some were, but others apparently were not; they came up any old way, hooked in the belly, in the gill, in the tail. Was it possible that all you had to do was drop a line to the bottom, give it a jerk and snag a cod? Was the bottom a solid carpet of fish, so that wherever you dropped a line, wherever any of these scores of boats dropped a line, it would hook a fish? The answers were evident all around us: we were in the presence of fish on a scale unimaginable, an unbelievable run of cod. While the run was on, every man and boy on the coast was out after them.

Codfish almost literally pave the shallower layers of the cold seas of the north at certain times of the year. It is not too much to say that they have had more to do with shaping the history of the modern world than any other living creature, barring man himself.

This needs some explaining. It requires a look back to the 16th and 17th Centuries, that extraordinary period when the countries of Western Europe exploded on a world totally unprepared to resist their fierce energies. What Portugal, Spain, France, Holland and England did during 200 years of exploration and empire building determined not only the political and geographical shaping of the globe during the three centuries that followed, but also the social attitudes that still energize Western civilization.

The fuel that fed much of that immense effort was the codfish.

The great thing about the cod was that it could be preserved. Either dried in the sun or salted, it was a perfect food to take on ocean voyages. The Portuguese, who were slowly edging their way around Africa and into the splendors of the East; the Spaniards, avid to find other treasure cities like those of the Aztec and the Inca; the pilgrims, the fugitives, the establishers of the colonies, the churchmen, the settlers, the traders, the soldiers who were needed to protect the newly carved empires from ravenous competitors—all could be fed on cod.

In the old days most cod fishing was done by hand line in several hundred feet of water. The men worked from dories, launched from the shore or from mother ships out at sea. It was a dangerous and brutal life. A day of hauling on long cod lines was backbreaking, and at day's end the offshore fisherman had to row back to his schooner—if he could find it. Storms were frequent, fogs more so. Often the mother ships were blown off station, the dories scattered for miles, and their weary occupants might row about for days, searching, before they perished from exposure.

The temperature of the water in these northern fishing banks has to be experienced to be believed. Much of the time it is only a degree or two above freezing and in summer the "warm" layers that the big cod like to lie in almost never go above 40°. Strangely enough, cod are sensitive to cold. Bring them suddenly from an environment of 40° water to one of 33° water and they start "shivering." Leave them there, and they may die. However, as the summer wanes cod adjust themselves to slowly lowering temperatures until they can endure water that is even a degree or two below freezing. But if a cod is suddenly yanked out of 30° water into 30° air, its eyes will begin clouding with ice crystals; soon the whole fish will be frozen solid.

Because of the cod's commercial importance, the Canadian government has studied the effect of concentrated modern trawling on the total cod population. Predictably, the trend is downward: this enormous resource is, thanks to the greed and foolishness of man, now beginning to be depleted. Annual yields of cod get smaller and smaller, as do the cod themselves, which no longer survive long enough to grow big. Today they average six to 12 pounds and live about five years. Thirty years ago they were twice that size and lived twice that long. Sixty-pounders were commonplace on the banks at the turn of the century, and there is a record of a 211-pounder caught in 1895.

The fate of the cod is shocking enough. But there is no better proof of the folly of short-term exploitation than in the rivers of this coast. Before they were befouled by chemicals discharged from riverside paper mills and factories, they swarmed with fish; they were the spawning grounds of sturgeon, striped bass, salmon and many other species. All of these are known as anadromous fish—those that live in salt water but come into fresh water to spawn.

The salmon is thought of today as a fish of the far north. That is where one finds it, in lands too bleak to support large-scale industry and where the rivers still run clean. Salmon were once common in the rivers of New England, but that was long ago, and the fish is largely unseen there now. What living American thinks of the factory-lined Housatonic or the Connecticut as a salmon river? Both once were. The same is true of the rivers of Maine.

Recently, I stopped on the bridge over the Androscoggin at Topsham, Maine. It is still a beautiful river, full of rocks and riffles and fast cold water from lakes far inland. It has deep pools, good sand and gravel bottoms, perfect for sturgeon, salmon or bass. But it is dead. Its waters are a brownish yellow and full of suds.

The condition of our rivers is too painful to linger over. It is a pleasure —no, a necessity—to drop downstream, away from the stench, the putrid oily sludge that gums their margins, out to sea again, to clean salt water. There one may encounter a creature that can easily be caught and studied: the lobster. And the ideal way to do this is to go out with one of that special breed of men from Maine and the Maritime Provinces of Canada who make their living from lobstering. If you haven't been out with a lobsterman on a fresh summer morning, you haven't lived. It makes little difference where you start; there are men all up and down the coast who, if properly approached, will be delighted—perhaps for a few dollars, perhaps only for the pleasure of a day's company—to have a passenger aboard as they work their traps.

I had a friend, now dead, who used to work the jumble of rocks and ledges to the west of Swan's Island in Maine. His name was Renfrew Wilberding. He was a short, stumpy, shiny-bald man with a face and neck of reddish-brown leather, bright brown eyes and callused hands so full of healed cuts from hauling lobster traps that they reminded me of snow tires. He wore a knitted green wool cap winter and summer. It hung on a hook inside the door of his house. He would put it on when he went out and hang it back on the hook when he came home for his supper. Over years at sea it became so caked with salt that in foggy weather it would quickly take up what must have been a quart of water.

"Be thick today," he would say. "My cap's gittin' heavy."

Ren's life spanned two worlds of lobstering. He went to work at the age of 13, at a time when lobster boats did not have engines. You rowed or you sailed, and you hauled every pot by hand. Later he turned to a modern powered boat. I went out with Ren more than once just for the joy of his company. But he was also a formidable source of lobster lore. He never stopped thinking about lobsters. He had a detailed picture in his mind of the two or three square miles of sea bottom that he regularly worked. I often think it was more real to him than the world of sun and fog and wind that he actually lived in. There was nothing that went on above the surface that he did not think about in terms of its effect on the hidden world below.

"Been blowin' too hard from the east," he might say. "Them big seas, they come rollin' in, they reach down, and them fellers on the bottom, they don't like that." For Ren, lobsters were sometimes "fellers on the bottom"; more often they were just referred to as "them"—he took it for granted that anybody would understand that sensible conversation had to be about lobsters.

I learned from Ren that a six-foot wave could be felt on the bottom in water that was 50 or more feet deep. This was the "reachin' down" that he often referred to, something that lobsters didn't like. "All that tuggin' and a-suckin' " made them sulky and they hid. Nevertheless, Ren made a point of going out right after a storm and checking all his pots.

"Stirs 'em up," he once explained. "Lobsters are too goddam lazy unless you stir 'em up once in a while."

How he reconciled these conflicting beliefs I never did learn, but I noticed that he drew imaginary lines around all the islands and ledges and never bothered to drop his traps in the shallow water inside them. He preferred to lay his string in water that was between 50 and 100 feet deep. Less than that, the "reachin' down" would pick up his traps in storms and smash them. Farther out, the cost of long lines to the pots and the time and energy required to haul them made lobstering unattractive—although there were "plenty of big fellers out there, down to two hunnert fathom."

That lobsters live at depths of more than a thousand feet I already knew. I had sailed across the Atlantic in 1957 as a member of the crew of the *Mayflower II*, a replica of the original vessel. Approaching landfall at the very end of our trip, somewhere off the Nantucket lightship, I woke one morning to the unfamiliar noise of boat engines. I ran on deck and found the *Mayflower* surrounded by fishing boats that were methodically dredging the bottom for deep-water lobsters. Having dined on one- and two-pounders all my life, I was unprepared for the monsters these boats were scraping up. The half dozen that were tossed aboard weighed between 20 and 30 pounds apiece. They had claws like baseball mitts and they had to be chopped in pieces before they would fit in the galley's largest pot. On the evidence of those mastodons I can testify that the flesh of a big lobster is no more coarse or tough than that of the tenderest chicken lobster. If anything, it has a sweeter flavor.

"I'll stick to chickens," said Ren when I told him about it. "Two chickens. Boiled. Nothin' better."

As he said this, we were headed out of Burnt Coat Harbor in Ren's boat, the *Dora W.,* named after his wife. It was 5 in the morning and almost pitch dark. The air was clear and cold, and as we passed under the blinking gleam of the harbor light, I huddled in the shelter of the cabin bulkhead and drank a cup of scalding tea. Ren finished his coffee and a doughnut and put his teeth around a large eight-cent cigar. He didn't light it. He just worked it around in his mouth.

Back of us in the cockpit were four lobster traps that he had picked up, broken, on his run two days earlier, mended the evening before, and would now return to the water. Each was a rectangular box made of wooden slats three feet long. Ren made all his traps himself, and was particular about their design. His had a funnel of netting going in at each end, terminating in a small hole.

"Five inches," he said, referring to the size of the hole in the netting. "There's some as go for four and a half and some as go for five and a half. Four and a half, the big fellers can't git in. Five and a half, too many little fellers git out. Five's right." He explained that the funnel of netting had to be nearer the top of the trap than the bottom and tilted upward, partly to make it more difficult for the lobster to escape, partly so that it couldn't reach in and grab the bait, which was fastened to the floor of the pot equidistant from either end.

Many lobstermen prefer a different design, with a single funnel entrance on the side. This is the so-called parlor pot, because that first funnel lets the lobster into an anteroom, or parlor, from which it then has to negotiate another net to get into the bedroom where the bait is. The rate of escape from parlor pots is lower than from the kind Ren used, but he stuck to his own.

"Them other kind are wuthless. Only one door. I got two doors. A lobster's pretty goddam dumb, and you gotta give him every chance you can for him to git in, then take your chance that he's too goddam dumb to git out. One door, he may never git in. One door, you might also git it plugged up with kelp. Then nothin' gits in."

So speaking, he slowed his boat down, baited one of the repaired traps from some very high-smelling fish in a small barrel, then slid the trap over the side. A long tethering line, or warp, followed it down. At the end of 60 or 70 feet of line was a stoppered bottle, and attached to that by another 10 or 20 feet of line was a top-shaped wooden buoy painted in Ren's colors, green and white, with a white handle. The double-float arrangement was to take care of changes in the tide.

The sun had now risen. It was a glorious morning, with air that made me stretch my lungs just to get another ounce or so into them. Ren had dropped the mended trap neatly between two of his green and white buoys that were about a hundred yards apart in what was otherwise an utterly featureless landscape.

"Good ledge down there," he explained. "Always keep a trap at each end, and drop one in the middle. Them goddam lobsters'r so lazy that maybe one of 'em won't take the trouble to walk that little extra distance. So I always drop one in the middle."

"How do you know where to drop it?"

"Like I say, right between them other two traps."

"But how about *them*? How do you know where the ledge is?"

"Well, it's right about here." He took off his green cap and rubbed his head. "You know, you walk out back to your privy a hunnert thousand times, you know where it is. You can git there with your eyes shut. Same with lobsterin'. You git to remember where things are."

During the morning Ren's uncanny ability at remembering was tested again and again. He dropped off his three remaining traps at precise locations. The rest of the day was devoted to checking half of the hundred or so traps comprising his set. The location of each pot was engraved in Ren's head, and the shortest distance needed to cover them all was the route he invariably traveled. As he approached a pot, he would throttle down, draw alongside, scoop the buoy out of the water and pull its line in hand over hand until he also had the glass bottle aboard. Then he would throw a couple of turns around the drum of a power takeoff from his engine. This drum was located at shoulder height at the after end of his cabin, and acted like a winch to pull up the trap. Except for the internal combustion engine itself, this one convenience has speeded up and eased lobstering more than anything else. Another recent improvement is the use of nylon line for warps and header nets. Otherwise, lobstering is conducted exactly as it has been for more than a century.

Ren's first trap came up with a rush. He handled the friction on the takeoff drum with one hand and swung the trap into the cockpit with the other with deceptive ease (I found it wasn't so simple when I tried it). As the trap came up, a couple of little crabs went flying out of it and some trails of kelp fell away. There was a good-sized lobster in one corner. Ren let the trap down on the deck, opened a trap door in the top, and reached in unconcernedly, paying no attention to the pair of large claws being waved at him. He picked the lobster up deftly by the back and held it down on the coaming while he fished in his pocket for a small peg that he stuck into the joint of the larger of the lobster's two claws. This forced the claw shut so that it could not bite—not for Ren's convenience, nor even ultimately for that of the housewife who would buy the lobster, but to prevent it from damaging other lobsters as he caught them. The pegged lobster was then tossed into a barrel of water kept fresh by a pump, driven by the boat's engine, that sluiced a steady supply of sea water into the barrel.

As Ren continued to haul in and check his traps, some came in empty, others contained several lobsters. Not all of these did he accept, however. Occasionally, when a trap held a smallish lobster, he would hook one end of a metal measuring gauge in the lobster's eye socket, and if the rear of the carapace—the heavy half cylinder of shell that covers the lobster's back—did not extend beyond the other end of the gauge, he would toss it back into the water.

"Short."

There are laws about catching lobsters. For example, in Maine and Massachusetts the law forbids lobstermen from keeping them unless the carapace measures at least three and three sixteenths inches. A lobsterman caught with "shorts" is fined and loses his license. Unlike other places, Maine also has a large-size limit. If the carapace is over five inches, that lobster also must be thrown back. One reason given for this is that larger and older lobsters usually produce more eggs.

At one point Ren tossed back a medium-sized lobster that looked perfectly marketable to me.

"Moltin'," he said.

He could tell from the deep red color around the lobster's joints that it was about to shed its shell. Since a lobster's flesh becomes stringy and watery just before it molts, it does not make good eating. Customers avoid molting lobsters, and Ren preferred to return them to the water, hoping to catch them again later.

"Why not let your buyer hold them in his pound until the molt is complete?" I asked.

"Wouldn't stick him with a molter," Ren replied. "Lobsters is cannibals. Nothin' they like to do more'n eat each other. Put a molter in a pound, them other lobsters would eat it soon as it shucked. My dealer'd be one lobster short."

Cannibalism, I reflected, was only one of the odd characteristics about this creature to which Ren had devoted his life. Even more curious is the way it reproduces. Its existence does not, as one might suppose, start when the male lobster impregnates the female. The male's sperm is stored in a small cavity on the underside of the female's body. There it stays until her eggs are formed, which may require a wait of nearly a year. The eggs are then squeezed out, being fertilized as they go, and are tucked in a mass—from 3,000 to 75,000 of them, depending on the age of the female—under her tail. They remain there, ripening, for nearly another year before they hatch. Being crustaceans, they go through larval and other stages of development, just as barnacles do, but in lobsters these changes occur inside the egg. The creature that finally hatches looks recognizably like an adult lobster, except that it is skinny, fragile, semitransparent—and less than a third of an inch long.

The fecundity of the lobster is offset by a high mortality rate; the rate of survival to maturity is believed to be about one in 5,000. The heaviest toll of baby lobsters comes during the first six or eight weeks of their lives, which are spent swimming freely in surface waters. Why, then, do they behave this way? Partly, it seems, because this is a way of ensuring that they will be widely distributed over the ocean floor; partly because during infancy they are themselves fiercely predatory on the smaller plankton that swim in the upper waters.

Whatever the reason, the survivors do grow rapidly. By the end of two months, having molted their shells several times and become about half an inch long, they have also abandoned the risks of the surface and have sunk to the bottom. There they spend the rest of their lives as prudently as possible, backed into cracks under rock ledges, hiding in weed beds, moving very little and mostly at night.

A year-old lobster will be three inches long and will have molted about 15 times. The molt itself is nothing short of a miracle. When its time comes, the lobster bends itself into a sharp "V" and its carapace splits cleanly up the back. It then proceeds to withdraw itself carefully from the old shell, every appendage down to the minutest hairs; even the surfaces of its multifaceted eyeballs are duplicated exactly by the new soft skin underneath; the long feelers are extracted, right to their very tips. The lobster then creeps away to hide and harden. As it does, its tissues reconstitute themselves into an individual that is 50 per cent larger than it was before the molt. Measuring a lobster against the shell it vacated a day earlier, one wonders how the creature fitted into it.

After its first year the lobster grows and molts more slowly. By the time it is five or six years old it will weigh about one pound and will be down to one molt a year. The big lobsters I encountered on the deck of the *Mayflower* were probably 50 years old. Still bigger ones are reported from colonial times, when lobsters were so abundant all along the coast that a dozen could be speared among the rocks in a couple of hours by an agile small boy with a sharp stick. New York Harbor, once one of the richest fish and shellfish centers in the world, is supposed to have yielded up an occasional lobster that was five or six feet long.

Estimates of the weights of those Goliaths do not survive, but the question of how big a lobster can get still persists. No one really knows. For crustaceans, as well as for fish, there seems to be no good reason why they should not grow indefinitely. They live in a stable environment, they are not overpowered by gravity as we mortals are, their metabolism is slowed by cold water and they do not seem to age. If they could get enough food, avoid larger enemies and resist parasites and disease, they might be able to live on and on. If a six-foot lobster, why not a ten-footer? "Dunno," Ren said. "Mebbe there are ten-footers. Never did see one."

By this time it was midafternoon and he had finished checking his set. His second cigar was shredding down dangerously small as we ran back to harbor and alongside the dock of his dealer. Tying up, he dumped his catch into a "car," one of a number of large oblong slatted holding boxes lying in the water at the wharf. The tide was out, exposing weed-covered rocks and long wharf pilings that were clotted by an indescribable jumble of marine growth. There was a strong sea-fish-mud-salt smell on the air, a good deal of it in my own clothes, thanks to a day's close association with Ren's bait barrel. He gave his lobster total to the boy who worked the dock, and we went up the slatted catwalk, which sank and rose with the tide. Although Ren was 78 and had been on his feet almost steadily since before sunrise, his step on the catwalk, now steep at low tide, was spry and quick. We shook hands and he went home to supper. Tomorrow he would be out again, and the next day and the next—as long as the weather held. By the end of November he would call it quits for the year, haul all his pots, get them in shape for the next season, and put them back into the water in March.

This last thing he never did. Three months later, he was out on a raw November day starting his year-end haul-out. It was sleeting and rough. Bringing up his second pot, he slipped on some ice that was forming in the cockpit, lost his grip on the power drum and fell to the deck; the 40-pound pot came down and crushed his hip. Somehow he lifted the pot off, got to his feet and, standing on one leg, managed to get his boat home. He spent three months in a hospital while his bones slowly knit, came home a tottery old man with a cane and died a month later.

Men against the Waters

No matter how remote or desolate, the earth's wild places have always drawn a hardy breed of men. From the first, the lure of the Northeast coast lay in the rich fishing grounds of the continental shelf—starting at the shoreline and in places reaching out to sea for hundreds of miles. Here, for almost five centuries, mariners from all parts of the North Atlantic have battled high winds and perilous seas to seek cod, haddock, pollock, halibut, mackerel and flounder. There have been herring fishermen and salmon fishermen, whalers and seal hunters.

In 1550, only five decades after John Cabot had crossed from England and first sighted the coast of Newfoundland, nearly 300 vessels from France, England, Spain and Portugal were reported offshore harvesting fish. Over the centuries since, huge fleets have fished a catch rivaling in value all the gold mined in North and South America. Even at the turn of the present century, when runs of cod and other groundfish were far smaller than they had been, the annual catch from New England waters alone seldom dipped below half a billion pounds.

Most of the wealth from the fishing industry has gone into the pockets of merchants and shipowners. For the seafarers, the enterprise has offered a life of unremitting hardship and danger: bitter January gales that drove ships aground, seas that swept men overboard into the icy ocean, and fogs into which dories disappeared forever. In his novel *Captains Courageous,* a tale of high adventure among the cod fishermen on the Grand Banks off Newfoundland, Rudyard Kipling set one year's death toll from a single fishing port at a hundred men and boys. The figure, though quoted in a work of fiction, was no exaggeration.

But for the seafarers, like those shown in the turn-of-the-century photographs on the following pages, the hazards and hardships were —and in a few cases still are —simply challenges to be overcome. Not many years ago, a 60-year-old Newfoundlander with leathery face and hands, who had begun fishing around 1900, spent a blustery January day hooking cod from his dory. At the day's end his shivering passenger, a landsman, cried out, "By God, it's inhuman for a man to have to get his living like this!"

"Not human, did ye say?" asked the fisherman in surprise. "Why, me dear man, 'tis the finest kind of life."

On a remote pebbly beach in Nova Scotia around 1915, two local cod fishermen clean their catch. A cod was usually dressed by being slit around the gills and from throat to tail; the innards were scooped out and the liver set aside for making cod-liver oil. Finally, with a single deft twist, the cod was decapitated, then split down the back to remove the backbone. The cleaned fish were packed in barrels with salt to preserve them.

Amid an organized clutter of spars, sails, bait tubs and fish lines, the crew of a 50-foot fishing schooner awaits a fair wind that will carry her from home port on Prince Edward Island to the cod grounds off Nova Scotia. In the foreground, the smallest hand performs the last of the dockside chores—the finicky task of baiting each hook on a 2,000-foot trawl line, which he coils neatly in a barrel so that it will run free when trailed over the side.

A day's fishing might consist of a
dawn-to-dusk coastal foray aboard the
boats at left, shown maneuvering off
Miscou Island in the Gulf of St.
Lawrence. Or it might take place 200
miles from land, in the Grand Banks
southeast of Newfoundland, where
fleets of dories are sent out each
morning from a mother ship that
cruises for months at a time. In the
dory above, two Banks fishermen pause
to check the day's catch—perhaps half
a ton of cod and halibut, pulled in on
the trawl coiled in a tub amidships.

The inhabitants of a 19th Century fishing settlement near St. John's, in Newfoundland, lay out salt cod for drying. The fish have already been cleaned and pickled in salt by the men who caught them; now, attended by the women and boys of the village, the cod must cure in the sun for about a month, spread out on crude wooden frames called "flakes" until they are thoroughly dry. Each evening the fish are taken up and stowed in sheds to protect them from dampness and then returned to the flakes the following morning for further drying.

Newfoundland whalers cut blubber from a fin-backed whale that has been herded into shallow water, then harpooned and towed ashore.

Newfoundland sealers (above) load pelts from a day's hunt onto a sledge, to be dragged across the ice to their ship. Crowding the ship's rail (right) to confirm a lookout's sighting of seals, hunters await the signal to leap out onto the ice. Seal hunts took place each spring during the whelping season on the ice packs off Newfoundland and Labrador. Fighting blustery March gales and arctic cold, in constant danger from the shifting ice, the sealers anchored amid the ice floes and set out on foot for the colonies of mother seals and especially their newborn pups, which they killed with clubs.

A Maine man, his boat lying grounded by low tide, rakes a rock-strewn stretch of sand and mud in search of clams for his supper.

5/ Warm Blood in the Cold Depths

There leviathan,/Hugest of living creatures, on the deep/Stretched like a promontory sleeps or swims,/And seems a moving land, and at his gills/Draws in, and at his trunk spouts out a sea.   JOHN MILTON/ *PARADISE LOST*

I have already mentioned a trip I took down the St. Lawrence in 1931 in a small ketch. At first we sailed along the north shore; passing the village of Tadoussac one evening, we ran beyond the ends of the roads and houses, down a dark coast where no lights shone. Here was true wilderness. The wind on the water was light, the air cold and fresh; a million stars were out; my three crewmates were asleep below. I sat alone in the cockpit, bundled in three sweaters, keeping the loom of the forested hills about half a mile off to port. There was no sound in that velvet dark, not even a bubble from the boat's wake.

Except . . . at intervals there would be a faint sigh, scarcely audible. At first I thought this noise was from the sleepers below, but I heard it again and again and finally realized that it was coming across the water, sometimes on one side of the boat, sometimes on the other. Suddenly there was a deep rushing breath right alongside that made me jump. I looked over the side. I either saw or imagined I saw a pale body arcing in the dark water. A porpoise, I thought, except that what I thought I had seen lingered strangely in my mind, as might a glimpse of a mermaid. This body appeared to have been white.

Porpoises are black, a rubbery shiny black. Could the starlight have been reflected by this body to make it look white? I had no other chance to tell. Nothing came close again, though the sighs continued, together with some extraordinary faint squeaks and muffled chirping sounds.

Again I tried to trace them to the boat, but I could not. They were coming from somewhere outside. Two hours later it was my turn to sleep, and I handed the helm over to a crewmate.

"There's a school of some kind of porpoises around here," I said. "They chirp."

"Come on!"

I was up again four hours later. Daylight had come.

"They're porpoises all right. Great big white ones. Look around you. They're everywhere."

As he spoke, one curved up about 50 feet away. It was white. It blew its quick wet sigh and curved down again out of sight. What we did not know and would not learn until later when we went ashore and inquired was that we had been sailing through a herd of beluga whales, a slightly larger relative of the porpoise and the dolphin, both members of the whale family.

The beluga is an arctic animal, never straying far from the southern edge of the ice sheet. Never, that is, except for one peculiar group of belugas that never leaves the St. Lawrence. There, apparently, the water is cold enough and the food plentiful enough for this herd to stay the year round. It has gotten itself wholly separated from the usual habitat of others of its kind nearer the North Pole. As far as scientists can tell, this group never mingles with other belugas at all.

When young, belugas are gray. As they grow they gradually turn yellowish, getting paler and paler as they mature. A full-grown beluga is a stunning sight—15 feet long, creamy white, with a blunt rounded head and a small myopic eye that can sometimes be glimpsed just as the animal surfaces. A beluga has no back fin, and its flippers and tail are rather small for its size. It is deliberate in its movements, giving nothing of the projectile effect created by its smaller kin, the dolphin, which seems to spray itself like a bullet through the waves of the open ocean.

All whales fall into two groups, those with teeth and those without. Both beluga and dolphin belong to the suborder of toothed whales known as Odontoceti, along with porpoises, narwhals, pilot whales, killer whales and the largest toothed creature in the world, the sperm whale. Size differences among the Odontoceti are remarkable. A common porpoise will run only four or five feet in length and 300 pounds in weight; a sperm whale may be 10 times as long and 300 times as heavy. The beluga falls in between, weighing up to 2,000 pounds. And it does chirp. In fact, it makes a great variety of squeaking, whistling and clicking sounds, which have earned it the name of sea canary.

The toothless, or baleen, whales belong to the suborder of Mysticeti. This is a group of generally large whales, formerly abundant in all the oceans of the world. Though reduced by hunting, most species are still found along the coasts of the United States and Canada. All but two of the Mysticeti reach 40 feet or more at maturity, with the blue whale running up to 100 feet and tipping the scales at up to 130 tons. This whale is by far the largest creature that has ever lived on earth, four times the weight of the largest dinosaur, 30 times that of an elephant. Taken together, all the men, women and children in my home town of Upper Brookville, New York (population: about 1,180), with their dogs and cats thrown in, weigh no more than one mature blue whale.

The large size of the baleen whales has to do with their feeding habits. They are, in effect, animated strainers, seemingly all mouth, which they open while swimming through the sea. Water flows into the front of the mouth as they swim, and out again at the sides, which are hung with curtains of baleen—long, stiff, springy fringed strands of whalebone, material similar to that which makes up hair and fingernails in other creatures. The individual baleen strips are far enough apart so that the water escapes through them, but close enough together to trap the small cold-water shrimp, or krill, that most baleen whales feed on. When a whale has swum through a thick shoal of krill, it pushes its tongue up to the roof of its mouth to force out any remaining water, then swallows the krill—thousands of them at a single gulp.

Here form and function have evolved together in a most interesting way. An animal that strains out such quantities of food obviously needs a large mouth—a strainer of maximum size and efficiency. Therefore the animal behind the mouth must be big to push it along. Also, it has to keep moving fairly steadily if it is to get enough food; it cannot, like a leopard, catch an antelope and live off that single kill for several days. Since constant movement burns up energy, this traps the whale in a circle of activity: the need to catch large numbers of krill to give it the energy to keep that large body moving to catch more krill.

If the problem were that simple, the whale's activity would seem to have a kind of desperate treadmill quality to it. But there are other factors involved. Cold water is rich water, and krill propagate in inconceivable numbers in arctic and antarctic seas. That is where baleen whales must go to eat them, and if they are to keep warm in that frigid water they must do something about it.

One thing they do is grow big. Since an increase in the size of an object increases its volume much faster than its surface area, it is clear that a large animal will lose heat through its skin more slowly—in proportion to its total body weight—than a small one. Therefore, it is greatly to the advantage of the whale with its cold-water problem to grow as big as it possibly can.

Another thing whales do is insulate themselves. This they achieve with layers of blubber under their skins. Blubber is sometimes a foot or two thick in the largest whales; it not only smooths and streamlines their bodies for most efficient movement through water, but also is an excellent heat conserver. However, it is never thick enough to be 100 per cent efficient. There is always some leakage of body heat, which requires the whale to be fairly constantly on the move in order to keep its body temperature slightly elevated to make up for that leakage.

For a mammal to live continuously in the sea, it must have a specialized skin, smooth and rubbery, to permit it not only to endure continuous exposure to salt water, but also to move through the water with a minimum of friction from individual water particles. A whale is a marvel of streamlining. Its nipples and sexual organs are recessed. It has no external ears, no hair, neither oil nor sweat glands. Since it lives in water there is no danger that its skin will dry out, and since the temperature of water does not fluctuate the way that of air does, a whale living a normal whale life does not have to worry too much from one day to the next about being too hot or too cold.

In addition to being smooth and tough, a whale's skin is remarkably insensitive. Many whales are infested with small crustaceans called whale lice, which get in the corners of their mouths, their genital slits and any cuts or abrasions that appear in their skins. For another animal, several hundred thousand large lice busily chewing away at its tissues would be maddening, but the whales seem unconcerned by their parasites, which is lucky since they cannot scratch themselves. Another nuisance is barnacles. A big sperm whale may lug around half a ton of them, some attached to its teeth.

Life for a whale starts after a fetal period of nine to 16 months. Babies are born tail first, as are many seals, although the general practice among mammals is a head-first delivery. The reason for the difference is that in these short-necked, large-headed seagoing animals the tail is much the most supple and slender part; delivery of that end first is easier on the mother. Eskimos believe that the tail-first delivery in belugas occurs to enable the calf to practice swimming for a couple of weeks before it is fully expelled from its mother. In fact, birth takes place quickly and the infant promptly swims to the surface for its first breath of air. If it does not do this, the mother may assist it to the surface; otherwise it will drown. Stillborn dolphins in aquariums have been observed being prodded anxiously to the surface by their mothers and by concerned "aunties," sometimes for hours.

A newborn nursing calf's next problem is to get enough milk during the half minute or so that it is able to stay under water. It does this by gripping its mother's nipple, whereupon a copious squirt of milk is shot into the baby's mouth, and it surfaces again. Whale milk is extremely rich, with a consistency close to that of condensed milk, and a taste reported by one adventurous expert to be a mixture of "fish, liver, milk of magnesia and oil." It is as rich as it is partly because the mother cannot easily spare the water for a weaker solution, partly because the calf is programed to grow so fast that it needs a concentrated diet. Blue whales that are 25 feet long and weigh two tons at birth grow at the rate of an inch or two and put on a couple of hundred pounds every day. Within six or seven months they are 50 feet long and weigh more than 20 tons—nearly half of which is head.

This awkwardly large head size presents problems in vision. The eye is located so far back on the side of the head that many whales cannot see forward at all. In addition, whales are probably nearsighted. Their eyeballs are rounder than is ideal for vision in a thin medium, air, to enable them to see better in a thicker medium, water. Although many of them are hunters, the evidence is that they rely less on their eyes to capture food than on echolocation. Their hearing is extraordinarily acute. Dolphins and porpoises—and probably the larger whales as well—find food by emitting very high squeaks, much as bats do, and homing in on the echoes that bounce off objects. Their ability to decipher these echoes is astonishing. A porpoise in a tank of water so muddy that it is totally opaque can discriminate—from the opposite end of the tank —between the shape of a fish that it likes to eat and one that it does not. A blindfolded dolphin can locate a BB dropped anywhere in its tank.

Whales are extremely intelligent, particularly the toothed whales. It is believed by many scientists that they are the smartest nonhuman animals on earth. Coupling that trait with their acute hearing, one might assume that they communicate by vocalization. It turns out that they do. Whales are great talkers, as has recently been demonstrated by recordings made of humpback whales in the waters off Bermuda.

I have a recording of those whale songs. They are without question the most extraordinary and haunting animal sounds I have ever heard.

Listening to them with stereo headphones, which is the way they *must* be listened to, brings the mystery and tragedy of the whale so close that it is almost unbearable. The stereo effect of the headphones conveys an uncanny sense of limitless expanses of water extending all around the listener. He becomes a whale, and it is his whale ears, designed to receive these messages from miles away—some claim hundreds of miles—that are ringing with the songs of great unseen creatures swimming out there somewhere in the darkness.

What are those whales saying? One voice will start with a couple of rising squeals that go up and up beyond human hearing, then return in echoes, in beautiful harmonics that do indeed sound like music. Is this a song, a lament or a complex statement of some sort? Who can tell? It is long-drawn-out and extraordinarily varied. It is interspersed by elephantine snorts and by put-put-put-put-put-put intervals that sound like a motorboat. This noise is followed by notes, deeper than organ tones, that are sensed more as vibrations of air than as actual sounds. Then comes a series of astonishing great whoops that start low and rise high as they go ringing out through the deep. They are so clear and strong, they convey so urgent a message, that the feeling of being a whale in the sea comes rushing in again, together with a terrible frustration born of an inability to understand and reply. It is simply unthinkable that soon this unearthly and powerful song may go unanswered in most of the oceans of the world, that tomorrow or the day after there may be no humpback whale outside northern waters to intercept this message and respond—for the humpback, like others of the large whales, has been ruthlessly hunted, and is now listed as a rare species requiring protection. It is to the credit of the Canadian government that the taking of baleen whales is now scrupulously regulated in Canadian waters. All species are making a small but highly encouraging comeback there.

The smaller toothed whales have never been systematically hunted, but that does not mean that they have been getting off scot-free. From prehistoric times men have been putting out in small boats to herd dolphins and porpoises into narrow estuaries from which they could not escape, setting nets in rivers and between islands. The pilot whale, or blackfish, travels in large schools in the North Atlantic. Every once in a while a bay in Newfoundland will suddenly fill with these whales, which have apparently rushed there in a panic. They either get themselves stranded in shallow water or mill around aimlessly until the delighted local fishermen can organize and drive the whales ashore. They are then slaughtered and divided up among the community. This is a windfall for the Newfoundlanders, who work harder and enjoy a lower standard of living than any other group of Canadians, but it is still an unpleasant business. The whales are frightened and defenseless, and when the grisly work is done, the waters of the harbor literally run red with their blood.

Why do pilot whales panic and rush inshore? There is no good answer to this question, particularly when one considers that the whales are highly intelligent and well able to take care of themselves most of the time. One suggestion is that when they find themselves in shallow water they become uneasy, swim about in increasing alarm—an alarm that is communicated rapidly, building up like crowd hysteria in human beings—and finally lose all good sense. There is reason for a whale to be afraid of shallow water. It can get stuck, and once stuck it runs a real risk of never floating free again. Furthermore, since the bulk of its body is accustomed to being supported by the water in which it swims, a large whale out of water suddenly finds itself burdened with a weight so great that it cannot breathe properly; its lungs are crushed by its own tissues and it suffocates.

Aside from the belugas and pilots seen in the St. Lawrence and off Newfoundland, the one species that the visitor to the Maritimes can almost surely count on meeting is the smallest whale of them all, the common porpoise. This rather shy creature will always keep a discreet 50 or 100 yards from your boat, and you always seem to glimpse it out of the corner of your eye just as it is curving down into the water again.

If you are luckier you will meet a party of dolphins. These are exuberant extroverts, common in the North Atlantic and far less diffident than porpoises. Dolphins are so high-spirited and cheerful, with built-in smiles permanently in place on their big turned-up mouths, that men have felt kindly disposed toward them for thousands of years. The Greeks liked them, and their literature is full of stories of nice dolphins that enjoyed guiding ships into harbors—stories that persist today and are at least half true. Dolphins also appeal to people today, with the notable exception of commercial fishermen: The animals get in their nets and do considerable damage. Newfoundlanders sometimes carry rifles in their boats and take pot shots at them. But no Newfoundlander I have met can match the experience of some Italian fishermen who accidentally netted a female dolphin in the Adriatic. Before she got loose their boat was nearly upset by other dolphins rushing to her rescue.

These animals were clearly responding to a distress call from the female, and were behaving as dolphins have often been observed to behave in captivity: they come to each other's aid. If one is injured or ailing, a couple of friends will get under it and hoist it to the surface so it can breathe.

Normal breathing for a dolphin—or any whale—is not difficult even though it is an underwater animal. The even distribution of its body weight, which permits it to lie horizontally in the water and thus swim with the least effort—also seems to have dictated the position of the blowhole on the top of the head. It was not always there. Once it was at the tip of the snout, in common with the nostrils of proper land animals. And this is a clear indication that whales are descended from such animals, instead of having evolved independently in the sea, as some people have argued. There is, in fact, abundant evidence to support the case for land descent. For one thing, fossils exist of what might be called semiwhales, with blowholes halfway back on their foreheads and skeletons whose flippers are more leglike than the flippers of today's whales. But even among these fossils the hind legs have entirely disappeared. Until we find an even older fossil that retains traces of hind legs, we must turn to the embryos of modern whales to find hints of their evolutionary descent. All whale fetuses when they are very young have four appendages that closely resemble the limbs that in other animals develop into legs. In whales the rear pair gradually disappears as the embryo grows, and the front pair turns into flippers. However, the flippers, which externally resemble paddles, internally have the bony structure of limbs. A whale's flipper contains all the arm bones that a man has, although in very distorted form. It also has five fingers, but again with a difference: the "thumb" has only one joint, whereas the longest finger has a dozen or more. These changes had already taken place in whales some 27 million years ago. True whales have existed all that time, although they once ran much smaller in size than they do today.

The need to breathe air regularly sometimes poses a special problem for whales in northern waters. The hazard of ice is hard to visualize during serene summer days in the Gulf of St. Lawrence, but in winter conditions are far different. The gulf produces its own ice pack, frozen surface water that is blown back and forth by strong winds, jamming, overriding itself, piling up into a thick jagged frosting, clearing leads of open water one day and then, on a shift of wind, remorselessly smashing them shut again. In this grinding turmoil, prudent whales keep off the edge of the ice pack. For a beluga, which can stay underwater for 15 or 20 minutes and swim a mile or two during that time, there is still the danger of finding itself suddenly walled off from its supply of air by five or 10 miles of unbroken ice; the ice pack moves about erratically in the gulf, and a section of coast that has been open and apparently safe for whales may be closed abruptly. The beluga has one special adaptation for such emergencies. In common with the right whale—also a polar species—it lacks a back fin. This enables it to bump its back against ice of considerable thickness in order to smash its way up for a breath of air.

The relationship between ice and certain seals is just the reverse. They need ice; they cannot keep away from it. For them, ice is a substitute for land, a place on which to give birth to pups and on which to rest while molting. The harp seal, the most common in Northeast coastal waters, is one such ice-bound animal. It is not well known to Americans, but is an important factor in the marine economy of the Gulf of St. Lawrence, where it spends a good part of its life and where Canadian sealers take a heavy toll of its pups.

A man tough enough to stand out on the very northern tip of Newfoundland in January, or in one of those desolate little rock pockets nearby like Nameless Cove or Savage Cove, will meet harp seals—if he does not become numb with cold and abandon the project. But the tearing winter storms and the frigid water do not bother the seals. Right after New Year's they begin pouring into the gulf through the Strait of Belle Isle. They have spent months at sea, ranging up and down the Labrador and Greenland coasts, feasting on fish. Now they are as sleek and as fat as butter. They frolic in, hundreds of thousands of them, frisking and skylarking as they come. For two months they feed in the gulf, then begin to gather on the edge of the ice sheet that has been forming like a big white scab along the shore, and that will gradually break off and move eastward to form a large clot in the center of the gulf just north of the Magdalen Islands.

The first seals to arrive at the ice sheet are the females. They cover it in huge patches, and during a few days they all give birth to pups. The babies, lying helpless on the ice, are lean at first, with no coat of blubber, but within a couple of days they begin to plump out on regular feedings of milk that is nearly 50 per cent fat, as compared to the 3.4 per cent fat content of cow's milk. The pups grow phenomenally; they must, for their mothers will nurse them for only three weeks. It is dangerous on the ice, and the time spent there must be as short as possible. They cannot be born right at the edge of the ice pack, in a kind of loose icy slush that is being sloshed and ground about by the waves; their mothers must deliver them farther in, on firm ice that will support the babies while they are growing. But not too far in—for that may involve too great a separation from the open water where the mother goes to feed. It may be beyond the ability of the mother to get to her baby to nurse if the open lead she has been using should be closed by ice movement. Harp seals are good at keeping open holes in the ice, through which they climb to nurse their young, but they are defenseless against major ice movements, and sealers often find terribly emaciated or dead babies whose mothers have had to abandon them.

Ice is always moving. If it is blown against the coast it will ride up over itself and may, in a single crunch, crush a dozen seal pups that are too roly-poly and helpless to get out of the way. Thick ice also supports the feet of men who come walking out with clubs. A newborn harp seal has, during the first week of its life, a lustrous, soft, pure-white coat that is "fast"—the hairs are firmly rooted in it and will not fall out. This coat brings a good price in the fur market, and the sealers walk rapidly among the pups, smashing in the skulls of any that have not started to molt. The blows are supposed to kill the pups; too often they are only stunned. The men are too busy cashing in on their windfall to stop to make sure. They want to get on to the next pup and the next before the ice is blown out to sea again. The result is a field of bleeding and dying pups with exploded eyeballs, crushed skulls and splintered jaws.

It takes a hard and determined man to kill a harp pup. It has enormous dark eyes, of a softness and gentleness and innocence that should abash any human being who pauses to look at them. A man has to step up quickly and swat the pup, ignore the brains that come bursting out and move on to the next victim. As the hunter approaches, the pup appears to know what is about to happen. It presses its foreflippers meekly against its sides, pulls in its head under a thick blubber-filled roll of skin around its neck, closes it eyes and waits for the blow to fall. Usually it is totally resistless.

So gruesome is the slaughter of harp seals that it has become a source of embarrassment to the Canadian government, which has imposed various humanitarian restrictions on the methods of killing. But it remains basically inhumane, whether carried out by men crossing the ice from shore or—more commonly—by men working from boats that enter the pack while it is out in the middle of the gulf. (The sealers, of course, argue thàt what they do is no more cruel than what goes on in slaugh-terhouses the world over.)

Two other kinds of seals that also occur in the Maritimes follow the same ritual of pupping on the ice. They are the gray seal and the hood-ed seal—though the gray often pups on land. Both are larger than the harp and much rarer. Oddly enough, however, the visitor's chance of seeing a gray seal—also called a horsehead because of the character-istic long sloping nose developed by the adult male—is actually better than it is for a harp. That is because grays summer in the St. Lawrence. They are found on Anticosti Island on the gulf's north shore, and are seen upriver as far as Trois-Pistoles. Anyone crossing the gulf in a boat in the neighborhood of the Magdalen Islands should certainly stop for a look at the colony of grays that always summers there. Grays also go out to sea through the Cabot Strait to the south of Newfoundland and make their way down the coast of Nova Scotia to the Bay of Fundy and the islands around Grand Manan. They get into the beautiful inland salt-water bays of Bras d'Or Lake, in the center of Cape Breton Island, and may occasionally be seen there, sunning themselves on rock ledges and unfrequented beaches. A tiny colony also persists on a sandbar at Nan-tucket off the Massachusetts coast.

But the seal that visitors will surely encounter, the seal that gives its name to Seal Cove, Seal Rocks, Seal Island and all the other seal-named spots that attest to its former abundance along the Northeast coast, is the common harbor seal. This animal is not ice-tied as the harp and hooded seals are, but gives birth to its pups on any secluded beach or hump of rock that it feels is safe. Of all the Atlantic seals, this is the one most closely tied to the land. As a result the life patterns that it has developed over many thousands of years in coping with large land pred-ators, and later with primitive human hunters, are different from those of the seals of the ice pack. Out there the harp pups are virtually im-mobile for the three weeks needed to stoke them up with enough growth and fat to make it on their own. This way of life, before the coming of man, was safe from everything but killer whales and ice movement. But harbor seals must be able to get into the water virtually at birth, if only to avoid drowning in the high tide that may cover the bar on which they were born. They are precocious swimmers, at home in the water almost from the first breath they take. One reason for this is that they are actually a little more developed at birth than harp seals. The "white coat" phase that takes place on the ice among harps takes place inside the mother among harbor seals. The pup is born as a "molter," grayish in color and with coarser hair.

This fact has saved harbor seals from concentrated hunting and almost certain extermination. As it is, they are shot regularly by fishermen, who know they are great fish eaters and do not wish to share the fish with the seals, and also because seals often get tangled in fish nets and tear large holes in them in their efforts to get free. Another problem that all Eastern seals have to contend with is that they are hosts to an internal parasitic worm that, in another phase of its life cycle, infests codfish and reduces their marketability. As a result, every fisherman's hand is against the harbor seal, and it has learned to be very wary of men in boats. I see them regularly among the rocks of the outer Maine islands, but never as close at hand as I would like. If I get too close they always slide circumspectly into the water and become sleek little heads bobbing up here and there in the distance.

To see harbor seals in action it is necessary to go to some place where they are not harried by people and—most important—where one can look almost straight down on them. One such spot that I know of is Matinicus Rock, at the mouth of Penobscot Bay, a few miles to sea from Matinicus Island.

The rock itself is a jumble of big granite blocks with colonies of arctic terns, razor-billed auks and puffins nesting in the crevices. Walk over to the ocean side. Pick the steepest clifflike spot you can find; lie down in a comfortable place with your chin looking over the edge of a rock, and wait. Pretty soon, in the waters below you, some dark heads will come along, diving and reappearing—a furry swirl zooming down and out of sight, a twist here, a dart of curling youngsters there. If the light is right, and if the water is truly calm, you may be able to catch glimpses of the seals beneath the water, tantalizing glimpses of a way of life you can only guess at.

The Seal Nurseries

PHOTOGRAPHS BY FRED BRUEMMER

Every February and March, certain icy and deserted places off the Northeast coast awake with raucous life: the region's seals have returned to breed. But though several hundred bulls and cows may cram onto a spit of land or an ice floe, they are rarely observed. In their evolution from land animals to creatures of the sea, seals have lost their four-legged mobility ashore; vulnerable, they choose the areas most inaccessible to predators in which to reforge their last unbreakable link to land—their need to breed there.

Of the 31 species of seals, three of the more elusive are the harp, the hooded and the gray. All three frequent this region's waters, and all three gather each year in rookeries scattered along the coast, or on the outlying ice pack.

Their annual reproductive rendezvous out of water are but a brief pause in the aquatic lives of these wide-ranging carnivorous mammals. Streamlined and insulated with a layer of blubber, seals swim with graceful speed despite their bulk (a hooded bull can weigh 900 pounds). Their hind flippers, encased in sleek coverings, can propel them at 15 miles per hour for short spurts.

As oceanic hunters of fish, squid and crustaceans, seals have evolved intricate mechanisms for conserving and consuming the oxygen in their blood. These give them an astonishing range underwater, enabling them to achieve depths of 600 feet while remaining submerged for as long as 30 minutes. So sophisticated are their respiratory and circulatory systems that seals can sleep underwater. When they need fresh air they surface without waking.

Yet the very traits that contribute to the seals' marvelous agility and grace at sea make them ungainly ashore. Unbuoyed by water, the seal finds its bulk burdensome; lacking jointed legs and feet, it humps along on land like a man in a sack race.

Thus the remoteness of their rookeries is the seals' chief protection against enemies. There is little the animals themselves can do, when ashore, to ward off determined human hunters. Only since 1964 has the government of Canada—where most seal hunting goes on—begun to place seals under protective legislation. These laws seem to have been enacted in time. But seals are still hunted and even those who seek to protect them disagree about quotas, slaughtering methods—and whether seals should be hunted at all.

Popping through a rift in the ice pack, a female harp seal warily scans her surroundings. Seals have good vision, especially when submerged; their large, wide eyes enable them to hunt for food even in deep water. Their eyes also account for their doleful expressions: because seals lack the ducts that in most mammals drain off the fluids that lubricate the eyes, tears flow ceaselessly down their faces.

Facing its mother across a channel of frigid water between ice floes (far left), a harp seal pup is momentarily separated from its food supply. Although the harp pup can swim almost from birth, its childhood is perilous: a pile-up of shifting ice can swiftly part it from its mother or crush it to death. At left, rejoined by its mother, the infant nuzzles, feeds and explores its snowy nursery. The pup's white coat serves as protective camouflage but ironically poses a special threat: prized by furriers, harp pup pelts are worth about $10 each to hunters who roam the ice with clubs during the pupping season. But if the baby seal can survive these hazards, it grows swiftly; doubling its body weight in two weeks, it sheds its fleecy coat in two more and takes to the ocean to hunt and swim on its own.

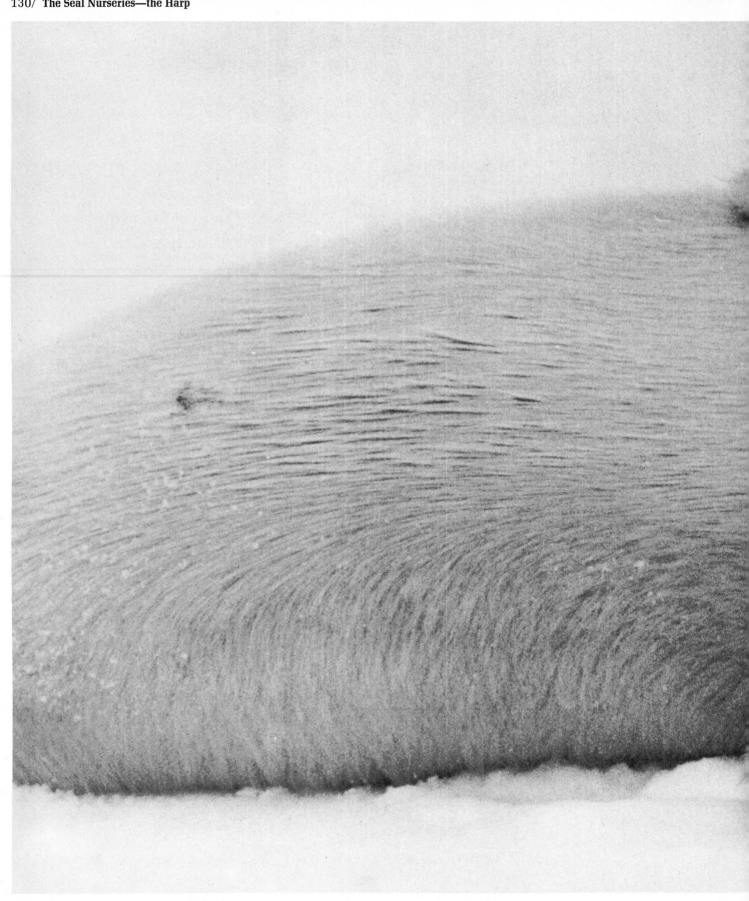

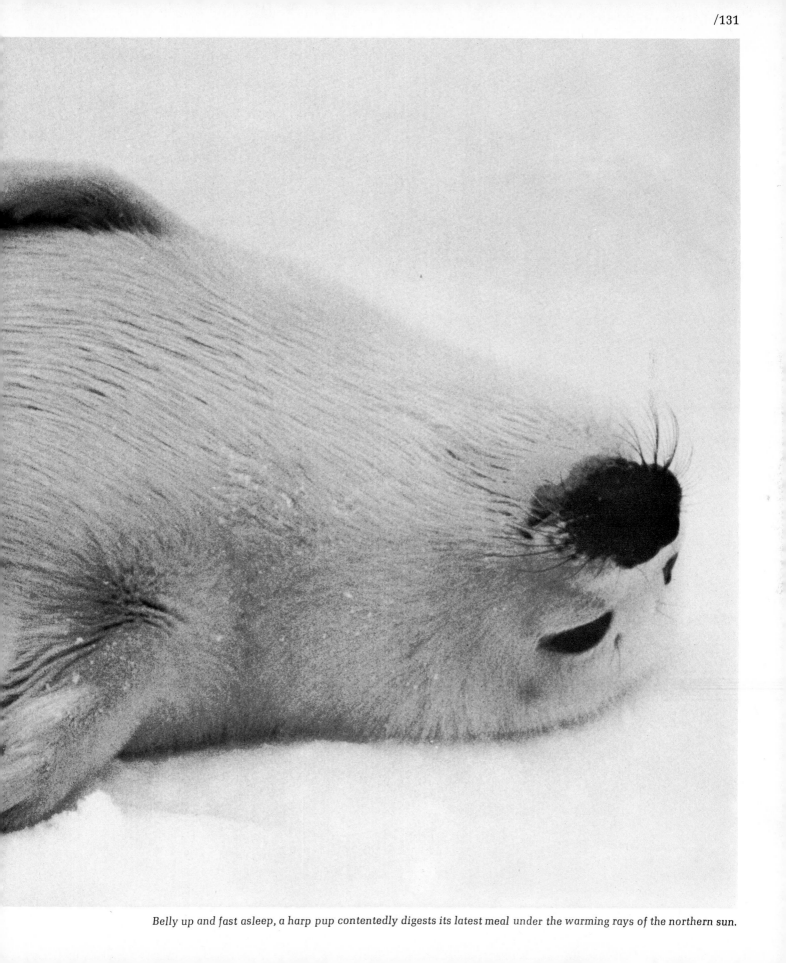

Belly up and fast asleep, a harp pup contentedly digests its latest meal under the warming rays of the northern sun.

With a menacing display of her sharp teeth, a surprised and enraged female hooded seal (left) warns an intruder approaching her newborn pup. Such invasions, however, are relatively rare events in the life of this species: hooded seals breed on ice floes —sometimes hundreds of miles from the coast—where the only visitor is an occasional polar bear or killer whale.

Squabbling about mating rights to a cow, two hooded bulls—each weighing nearly half a ton—tilt through icy slush, their inflatable noses fully erect. The balloonlike appendage for which the species is named is found only on males. When a bull becomes excited, the hood expands to about twice the size of a football, deflating—when he calms down—with a resonant "pop."

Strewn like sausages amid a clutter of wrecked lobster pots and other driftwood, a colony of gray seal cows and pups takes the sun on Basque Island near Cape Breton, Nova Scotia. Though the species ranges from Labrador to Nantucket, grays are infrequently seen except in their St. Lawrence-area summering grounds. Not only do they breed on isolated islands and pack ice, but the number of grays in the region is estimated at only 10,000 to 15,000. Still this represents a giant leap from the 5,000 reported just five years ago. Whether the grays are indeed increasing or man's spotting methods are improving, even the experts can't say.

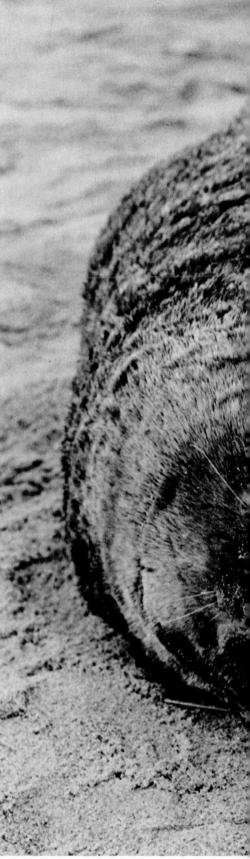

Startling his chosen consort, a bull gray seal pins a lighter-colored cow to the ground before mating with her. His sudden possessive gesture ends a long pursuit: for two weeks he has been staking out his territory and lining up his harem. The cow, busy giving birth and nursing her pup, has rebuffed him several times. But now, with her mothering duties over, the cow submits and the courtship is consummated.

In a close embrace, the bull and cow lie on the sand and mate. The result of their brief meeting will be a 30-inch-long pup, which will be born weighing about 35 pounds and covered with long, creamy white wool. Within days of mating, both adult seals will rejoin the rest of their herd in the sea. There they will remain, returning a year hence —probably to this same remote island in time for the cow to bear her pup.

The Bird Cities

Considering the nature of the Northeast coast, this book has, of necessity, dealt extensively with islands. By design also, for I love islands. Their very separation from the mainland, their quiet and serenity, their unclutteredness, the purity of their air, the constant presence of the sea around them—all of these things draw me to them.

But beyond personal sentiment there is a better reason for looking at the Northeast islands.

There was a golden time—after the glacial ice left and before men came—when many of these were densely inhabited by birds. A few of these throbbing, whirling bird metropolises survive intact, and my greatest reward in writing this book has been the opportunity to visit some of them and to learn something about the intricate lives that their denizens lead. What follows is an informal journal of experiences on a recent early summer trip I made to three such spots.

Kent Island

I am accompanied by my wife, Helen, and a relative, Christa Armstrong. We have flown from Boston to Saint John, New Brunswick, and from there down to the mouth of the Bay of Fundy to Grand Manan Island, a beautiful and rugged place 10 miles off the coast, almost directly opposite the border between Maine and Canada. Now we must take a boat to another much smaller island, a mere sliver that lies still farther out to sea.

"Going to Kent Island?" asks our taxi driver, Mrs. Green, looking at our mounds of sleeping bags, duffel bags, camera bags and tripods.

"Yes."

"Pretty place."

"You know it?"

"Oh, yes. Used to go egging there when I was little. Gull eggs make the best angel cake. Better than any chicken."

"Gull eggs? Do they taste good?"

"Oh, yes. Look kind of funny poached, though. Yolks are red. Whites are green."

She drives us to a wharf. Moored alongside is a lobster boat twice the size of those used in Maine, and equipped with a radar antenna. I note this with relief, for the fog is so thick that we can scarcely see to the end of the wharf.

We meet the boat owner, Myhron Tate, who in addition to his regular work as a lobsterman provides a marine taxi and supply service for Dr. Charles Huntington, a biologist from

LORD OF THE COAST: THE EVER-PRESENT HERRING GULL

A GULL ALERT FOR PREY

Bowdoin College in Maine. Bowdoin owns Kent Island, and Chuck Huntington directs a summer program there for biology students, meanwhile continuing his own ornithological research. Chuck is a world authority on petrels.

Myhron puts several large boxes of groceries in the cockpit. We dump in our gear. All is covered with a tarpaulin, and off we go into a wall of dripping clammy white. The radar is immediately switched on.

Forty minutes of nothing. Then I notice a faint shadow nearby, a weed-covered ledge. The fog lifts a little. Some slats of a fish weir appear. Myhron throttles down and noses us through a narrow channel and up to a small wharf. The outlines of some trees rear up. Out of the mist come Chuck Huntington and three students, down a path to help us unload. It is a quarter of a mile up through a meadow and along the edge of some woods to the camp. We

lug as much of our stuff as we can carry. The rest is trundled in a wheelbarrow by Charlie, a husky young student. We meet others, Todd, Jed, Mark, John—also Judy, Jacquie, Sherry, Pam and Carolyn. Five college girls, five boys, each working on a project. Today they are little more than a blur of strange faces. A week later, when we leave, they will have become friends.

Fog everywhere. A ghostly gray building emerges in a clearing. A tent. A privy. Another building. Here we will stay, Helen and I in sleeping bags in a room next to the main dining and social room, Christa upstairs in the girls' dormitory.

Our first day is devoted to getting acquainted with the island. Kent is only about 200 acres in size, but it seems much larger because it is long and thin, and provides a rough walk of two miles from one end to the other. Ornithologically the island has three distinct specialties: herring gulls, American eiders and Leach's petrels. All breed here in large numbers, but only gulls are visible. They are everywhere, perched on the shore, in trees, on fish weirs, on the shacks. They fly tirelessly. Their cries are continuous, from the little "kuk-kuks" of alarm that they utter, seemingly talking to themselves, to the long mournful screams I have always associated with waking up in the morning by the sea.

Chuck Huntington cautions us. "When you walk down to the shore, please be careful. If an eider is taking her ducklings to the water, back off so that you won't scare her away

SUN-GILDED EIDER DUCKS OFF KENT ISLAND

from them." I promise. I already know that herring gulls prey on little eiders, which are doomed if they are separated from their mothers.

On Kent Island many of the eiders nest in the woods, deep among the spruces, hidden away from the sharp eyes of the gulls. The nests are neat and round and about the size of a soup plate; they are lined with a thick layer of soft gray feathers —eider down—plucked from the mother duck's breast. As we crawl through the woods, we find many such nests, some untenanted, others with broody ducks sitting on four large green eggs. Over and over we suddenly come upon a soft brown back scarcely visible in the surrounding forest litter, a curve of head and neck, alert but motionless, a bright black eye. Sometimes, as we approach, the duck will leave the nest and waddle silently away in the undergrowth. A moment later we will hear her take off, blundering and crashing through the trees. Eiders are heavy-bodied birds. They are fast but ponderous fliers. Tanklike, they travel in straight lines until well airborne. It is a mystery how, in emergencies, they can beat their way out of the forest tangle they live in without damaging themselves.

Sometimes, if her eggs are just about to hatch, a duck will sit fast. You can put your hand on her, feel her heart beat, look right into that wild watchful black eye.

Trying to find the shore, we follow more than one path through the woods, scaring up a couple of eiders as we go. Suddenly the path ends in a strip of marsh with the salt water just beyond. Right in the path is a two-foot puddle and in the puddle is a mother duck with four just-hatched ducklings. We stop. Mother and babies retire into some deep grass. We give them a few minutes, then make a detour around them to the beach. Here, just above high-tide level, is a low barrier of storm-tossed driftwood and hummocks of beach grass. Perched at intervals on this barrier, like tax collectors and just as cold of eye, are the gulls. They are waiting. Sooner or later a duck will take her babies to the water.

As we watch, the mother that was in the puddle a few minutes ago decides to make her run. Fifty feet down the beach she suddenly appears out of the grass, walking fast among the slippery stones, her babies racing behind, tumbling, sliding, crowding against her. Instantly the gulls gather, screaming, and begin

their dives. She rears up, fending them off with her bill. She reaches the water. The little ones begin frantically swimming. Three gulls swoop and a laggard duckling is neatly picked like a bug from the water. The last we see of it is two tiny webbed feet splayed against the sky.

The mother has whirled too late to save this one; she leaves the others unprotected. They have never swum before, never dived before, but they dive now. All three vanish. But they must come up in a few seconds. As they do, two more are immediately snatched by the hovering gulls. Only one duckling surfaces near enough to the mother to swim with her to deeper water and the safety of a flock of adult ducks.

This brutal harvest has taken 10 seconds. It is over while we are still trying to comprehend it. Three gone out of four. What a terrible toll. Were we in any way responsible?

"No," says Chuck later. "The mother may have been young and inexperienced, or just unlucky. I have no figures on the actual number of young ducks that make it safely, but I would guess that about half do. If they stay close, the mother can usually defend a couple of ducklings with her bill. Once she gets them out there with the other adult ducks, they're not in much danger."

The fog persists. It drenches everything. I spend the next day trying to make pictures of tiny flowers, mosses, tree buds and cobwebs, each carrying a heavy freight of fog in minute glittering droplets. No wonder everything is so green and lush here. No wonder things rot so fast. When the spruces die and fall they quickly disintegrate, swallowed by the mosses and ferns that make soft burial mounds over the crumbling bones that were their branches. What is decaying wood, what honest-to-goodness soil and what growing leaves is hard to tell. There seems to be no clear boundary between ground and plants. The footing is extraordinarily spongy and springy. Once or twice I go right through the surface of the ground, up to my shin. I have broken through a crust into a hole of some kind—or so I think, and this is confirmed by Chuck Huntington. He says I may have stepped into a petrel burrow.

I have already noticed small red tags hanging from spruce branches here and there in the woods. They have been put there over the years by Chuck and various assistants. Each tag marks the location of a pe-

A DOWN-CUSHIONED EIDER NEST

FOR SAFETY'S SAKE: EIDER DUCKLINGS HUDDLING NEAR MOTHER

trel burrow. One afternoon we go down where the tags are to check the burrows. Pam is Chuck's helper in this work. She enters all pertinent data on each burrow in a large notebook as Chuck makes the rounds. A Swainson's thrush warbles somewhere; otherwise there is absolute stillness. The spruce grove seems utterly lifeless—except for the message of those red tags. They remind us that down in the ground beneath our feet is an unseen, silent, unsuspected population of birds crouching in a veritable honeycomb of burrows. This seems unbelievable, the more so when I reflect that petrels are pelagic birds, miniature cousins of albatrosses, that spend their lives on the wing far out to sea. But they are here now, breeding, all around us, and Chuck will soon prove it. He sits down in a fern bed and we settle ourselves opposite him.

"The fifth best way to get a petrel out of a burrow," he says, "is to pull it out backwards by the tail."

We learn that the best way is to get your hand gently around the petrel's neck and body, and draw it out headfirst. Never pull it out by a leg. This may injure a wing or break some flight feathers, and a petrel that cannot fly properly cannot live.

"Okay," says Chuck, "where do we go first?"

"Number two hundred and six," says Pam, consulting her notebook.

"Two oh six. Let's see." He hesitates a moment, then turns three feet to his left and brushes back a spray of ferns with his hand, revealing an inconspicuous hole in the ground about three inches across. He flops on his belly, shoves his arm in the hole almost up to his shoulder, then gently draws it out again. Held between thumb and forefinger by the tip of its bill—the second best method—is a smallish sooty bird with a white rump. It has a curved black bill, a black eye, black legs and delicately webbed black feet. It lies

A LEACH'S PETREL SOARING SEAWARD

quietly on its back in Chuck's hand, and makes little swimming motions with its feet.

"No band," says Chuck. "A new bird." He gently clamps a small Monel metal band to its leg with a pair of pliers. He reads the band number aloud. Pam records it.

"Now for the egg."

Instead of reaching into the burrow entrance again, Chuck pries up a square of turf that he has previously cut directly over the nest in the back of the burrow. The turf

rests on an old shingle that fits neatly into the ground like a trap door, providing a convenient way to gain direct access to the nest. He kneels down and looks in.

"Egg," he says, and Pam writes.

He then carefully replaces the turf square. "I always do that before returning the bird, and I always let the bird go back in through the front door. That way, she doesn't even know the trap door is there, and it doesn't interfere with her nesting." The petrel is released in front of the burrow. It quickly scuttles in out of sight. Chuck then carefully props up a few small twigs in the burrow entrance. A bird coming or going will have to shoulder the twigs aside, and on his next visit Chuck will know the burrow is being used.

"Lattice in place. Next."

"Number eleven," says Pam.

"Eleven. Eleven is a very interesting burrow," says Chuck. "Last year a bird was in it that I banded as a breeding bird in 1953. It has been in this burrow almost every year since then. Since it had to be at least four before it was old enough to nest, that made it at least 21 years old last year. Maybe older, because we don't know how many years it had been here before we first banded it."

Number eleven proves to be occupied. Another record—the bird in it is now at least 22 years old.

"Next."

"Seventy-three."

Down Chuck flops once more. "Seventy-three is unoccupied. Lattice undisturbed."

So it goes through a long afternoon. I can scarcely get it through my head that this quiet spruce grove is the roof of a swarming bird city, tunneled like a gigantic anthill, that there are hundreds of petrels down there, safe in the holes they have either inherited from departed ancestors or dug themselves by lying on

their sides, industriously excavating with their bills, shoveling out the loose dirt with their feet. How have they come to this island? How is it that they are never seen? Why isn't the sky full of petrels coming and going all day?

"Herring gulls," explains Chuck.

The petrel, being small, inoffensive and specialized for overwater flight, is easy prey for a gull over land during the day. As a consequence, it can safely come to shore only at night.

Petrels arrive at Kent as early as April, when there is still ice in the burrows. They must come early, for they have a long season of work ahead of them. Most small land birds, like robins, blackbirds or sparrows, can lay eggs, raise nestlings and kick them out into the world in a little over a month's time. A petrel needs four months to do the same job. Although its body is no bigger than a catbird's, it lays an egg twice the size of a catbird egg. This unusually large object is then incubat-

BUNDLE OF FLUFF: A NEWBORN PETREL

ed for about 42 days. While one of the parents broods the egg the other is at sea, feeding. After three or four days it will return at night, drop to the ground and crawl into the burrow to join its mate. They may spend some time there cooing and purring to each other, but before daylight the relieved partner will depart for its turn to feed at sea.

When the chick hatches it is fed with regurgitated food throughout the summer and on into the fall—for a total of 60 days or more—until it is fully grown and much fatter and heavier than its parents. Now the reason for its long period of development is made clear. One night the parents abandon it—forever. The chick crawls to the mouth of the burrow, anxiously, hungrily and hopefully. Nobody comes to feed it. It flutters its wings a few times experimentally. Daylight comes, and it creeps back into the safe darkness. A night or two later, it makes a short trial flight for only a few minutes, but somehow finds its way back to its burrow in the dark. Then, when its weight has dropped to just a few grams more than that of its parents, it takes off, goaded by hunger. Guided by instinct, it heads out to an ocean that it has never seen and does not know exists; it will learn to feed on small surface fish and planktonic creatures that it has never encountered except in digested form, and whose whereabouts and habits it is totally ignorant of; it will use its eyes to make its living in the sun although it has grown in darkness.

Our petrel day is not over. Around

10:30 p.m., we fumble our way back to the spot where earlier we had been opening burrows. It is totally black in here. The ferns can only be felt and smelled, a cloudy, foamy fragrance brushing my face as I crouch among them.

"Hear anything?" asks Chuck.

I lie down and put my ear to the ground. From beneath me come the voices of petrels purring—a gentle, sustained, contented mutter from two birds that are enjoying each other's company for a little while before they separate again. What a strange and wonderful utterance. Springing from the dark earth, it seems to speak for all the mystery of these extraordinary little birds. Lying there listening, unwilling to tear myself away, I wonder if stories about elves and other small people of forest glades may not have been launched on the purring of petrels.

Great Island

Helen, Christa and I have flown another 700 miles north and east, and are now in St. John's, Newfoundland, a colder and wetter place than the one we have just left. A road runs south down this coast, skirting a succession of bays, into each of which is tucked a small fishing village with its harbor.

We arrive at one of these—Bauline East, about an hour's drive south of St. John's—around 9 o'clock on a gusty morning with rain squalls scudding past. The fishermen have been out since 5, and they are now coming in, hoisting boatloads of cod onto the dock, where the fish are quickly dressed by other men stand-

ing at slimy tables in oilskin bib overalls. Squatting nearby is a woman with two piles of small bloody carcasses in front of her. She reaches behind her for something—the black-and-white feathered body of a bird. She cuts off its head, skins it deftly and with extraordinary speed, and then reaches for another. I recognize the birds as murres and, knowing that they probably come

A WELCOME FOR A PUFFIN PROVIDER

from an island sanctuary nearby, I ask her how she gets them.

"They coom up with the cod in the nets. They doive, y'know, and get caaght in the nets."

"Do they taste good?"

"Sure, they do. But these here" —she gestures toward her second and smaller pile—"these ain't so noice. Tough, y'know. Have to bile 'em good." These other birds are puffins, as I recognize from the thick parrotlike red-and-yellow bills on their severed heads.

It is puffins that we have come to Bauline East to see. Offshore, a couple of miles away, veiled in rain squalls, is their home, Great Island. From here it looks like a steep-sided rock gumdrop, half a mile across. Our transportation to the island has been arranged with a fisherman named John Reddick, and we are waiting now on the fish wharf for Reddick to come in with his boat.

Eventually he does. He is a strikingly handsome man with bright blue eyes, who tells us that there are two young lady biologists camped out on the island.

By now the wind has died down. In Reddick's "one-lunger" we pop-pop-pop out across the swells of an oily sea. The closer we get to Great Island, the more we become aware of the clouds of birds flying around it, and of the battalions and brigades sitting on it.

Reddick cuts his motor and his boat sidles into a deep crack between two rocks. There is a bright yellow nylon rope hanging down one of them. Although this is probably the calmest day of the summer, there is still a sea surge that sends the boat slowly up and down. As the bow rises, one is supposed to grab the rope and step off onto the rock, then pull oneself up about 20 feet to a tufty grassy platform above. I look up. Two puffins sitting there look down at me. The boat rises. I step off. Easy! Our cameras and tripods are handed ashore. But getting up the rock isn't so easy. It is still raining, and the bird guano that is spattered everywhere is as slippery as soap.

FILLING THE BILL: A PUFFIN'S PROUD CATCH

Eventually Helen, Christa and I —with cameras—make our way up to the grassy plateau. We look around us at a miniature landscape, the like of which I have never seen before. It consists of nothing but bumps, large hummocks of thick grass interspersed everywhere with holes, as if an army of woodchucks lived here. This is a puffinry, a Swiss-cheese land, more air than soil. The diggers—the puffins—stand all around, solemnly observing us.

A puffin is a hard bird to describe. Its physical appearance is so bizarre that one is at first wholly preoccupied with this. It is only after the shock of looking at it has worn off somewhat that one begins to realize that the puffin personality has just as strong and hilarious an impact as its appearance.

A puffin is an alcid, a member of the same family as the auks. Like the auks it bears a vague resemblance to a penguin. Its shape is portly. It stands upright on a pair of bright red or orange feet located well aft under its tail. Its wings are small and stumpy, reflecting a way of life in which underwater swimming (with the wings, not the feet) is as important as flying. Other alcids—razor-billed auks, guillemots and dovekies—are similarly stub-winged, and sometimes when the sea is flat and there are no waves to help fling them aloft, they find it almost impossible to get airborne. It is conceivable that an alcid species might eventually lose the power of flight altogether. This is what happened to a larger relative, the great auk—and that fact is mainly responsible for its extinction. Because it could not fly, it could not escape its human predators, who hunted it for meat and plumage. Funk Island, which once had a population in the millions, is only 175 miles or so up the coast from where we now sit on Great Island, contemplating the little cousins of this vanished auk. I cannot help wondering if some accident, some quirk of human need or greed may eventually do the puffin in. For it, too, is vulnerable—to cats or rats if they by chance should get on Great Island, to humans who might decide that puffins are not as tough eating as the dockside lady claimed, to an influx of bird watchers who plod heavy-footed among their burrows, to oil slicks that kill all sea birds.

These gloomy thoughts about the irreversible nature of extinction are hard to sustain in the presence of the puffins. They are preposterous birds. Their formal attire of black tail coat and starched white shirt front, their upright stance, their self-important bustle—all suggest small dignified headwaiters who, for some eccentric reason of their own, have decided to wear enormous false clown noses painted bright yellow and red.

It is this duality of appearance that makes puffins so intriguing, the more so because it is carried over into their behavior. Puffins are alternately intent on their own affairs and comically concerned with the affairs of their neighbors. One moment they will be bringing fish for their young, vigorously kicking dirt out of their burrows, flying busily about like oversized bumblebees; the next they will drop everything to gawk at what somebody else is doing. If two puffins rub their bills together as a sign of affection or sexual attraction, the neighbors will gather to watch.

All this we see around us. We are on the edge of a small grassy bowl, in the midst of some five hundred or a thousand burrows. The occupants of the nearest ones have retired discreetly to a rock ledge over the sea to wait our departure. The others pay no attention to us at all. Puffin life, in all its solemn efficient absurdity, is going on at a busy clip everywhere. And in complete silence. Unlike most other sea birds, puffins do not talk. Only when disturbed or in their burrows do they say much, and then they growl.

The longer one stays to watch in this thronging community, the more one begins to see. My eye is on one burrow from which shovelfuls of earth are flying. Suddenly the housekeeper appears, turns around so that her tail is facing outward. Splat! A jet of guano is ejected downhill with enough force so that the area closest to the burrow entrance—the front yard—is kept clean.

Having attended to her business, the puffin housewife trudges back into the burrow. A moment later somebody who must be her husband arrives. He barrels in in a high-speed stall, wings fluttering, feet splayed for braking. He crash-lands, tumbles forward on his chest in the grass, but does not lose his grip on seven fish he is carrying in his bill. He scuttles inside. Obviously there is a chick in there, but I am not about to put my hand in to investigate. That big bill has the force of a wire cutter.

That the puffin can fly about underwater at top speed, grabbing fish without losing others it has already caught, is remarkable. R. M. Lockley, a world authority on puffins, explains that the first fish caught is given a sharp bite that instantly kills it. It is then transferred to the rearmost part of the bill, which does not need to be opened wide as its owner snaps at other fish. Gradually the back of the bill gets filled up and the load would become unmanageable except that the upper mandible has a rough sawtooth edge that provides a grip for fish that are farther forward. It is nothing to see a bird holding a dozen dangling capelin. Lockley has counted as many as 28 being held in one bill. He has also observed rogue herring gulls that have learned a technique of jostling the puffins as they come in for a landing. This sends them tumbling, the fish they are carrying go every which way, and the gulls gobble them up.

A more serious menace is the great black-backed gull. This is the largest and most powerful of all gulls, and it preys on puffins. It will settle in the midst of a puffin colony and wait patiently, appearing to be half asleep. The puffins are wary of it at first and keep a sharp eye on it. After a while, however, one will be lulled into inattention. The gull will strike, seizing the puffin and carrying it off.

Walking here is just about impossible. I slide and flounder among the tufts, trying to avoid four burrows,

A PUFFIN COLONY ON THE HUMMOCKS OF GREAT ISLAND

only to go crashing into a fifth. The owner comes bolting out, flapping madly, bounces on the grass, turns three somersaults down the hill, finally disappears over a cliff, still trying to get itself properly airborne. The footing is made particularly difficult because, in addition to the large and obvious puffin burrows, there are innumerable petrel burrows here too. I ask one of the girl biologists who are camping out on the island about them.

"Oh, yes," she says. "There are more petrels here than anything else. You should see it at night. Like moths, they are. I was out walking the other evening. I opened my mouth and one flew right in."

"Into your *mouth?*"

"Yes. It flew out."

She takes me back to the little hut where she and her assistant are living and makes me a cup of tea. The assistant is very fidgety. It turns out that she is squeamish about ticks.

"Ticks? Here?"

"Oh, yes. Puffins are bothered by ticks. Sometimes their faces are covered with them."

That night back in St. John's I find that I have brought a souvenir of Great Island away with me. Taking a bath, I find two ticks on my thigh.

Cape St. Mary's

We are up early because there are a hundred miles of bad road between us and our destination, a headland near the southern tip of eastern Newfoundland. At last we turn off onto a tiny road that leads across a moor to a lighthouse at the top of a headland overlooking the sea.

A MURRE MOTHER AND HER CHICKS

The view alone is worth the ride. Other headlands stand along the coast like buttresses of a mammoth church. They have rounded grassy summits that fall off into vertical faces of rock 500 feet high. Deep cracks and gorges separate them. We can edge our way out and look down into these, and across the way at the facing cliffs. Here is another fantastic bird society composed of kittiwakes and murres, the former a gull, the latter an alcid, with the alcid's dark head and back and white underparts. Like puffins, the murres are short-winged ocean dwellers that come ashore to these towering cliffs only for nesting.

For a murre, however, the word nesting is an exaggeration. It lays its single egg on bare rock, often on a ledge only a few inches wide. The egg is pointed and heavier at the small end, so that if moved it will roll in a tight circle, lessening the chance that it will fall off the ledge.

Murres are the most sociable of the alcids. They gather for breeding wherever there is flat space for them to sit, clustering there in dense concentrations of about one bird per square foot of sitting space. There is a constant change of personnel on a crowded ledge below us. Murres come swinging in from the sea, their stumpy wings pumping as fast as those of puffins. They aim themselves right at the rock face, at a point a few feet below the ledge, coming in at suicidal speed. At the last moment they veer upward, losing speed and plopping clumsily on the ledge to a noisy chorus of

"arrrhhs" and snakelike bobbing heads. Sometimes there is no room for the arriving bird. It flutters and tumbles off, regaining its balance as it falls, and goes zooming off to sea to circle around and return to try for a landing again.

I get a sense of mindless fecund confusion among murres, as if they were out to defeat the forces of accident and predation by sheer weight of numbers. Where humans do not interfere, murres bloom like algae in their huge northern colonies, known as loomeries. The Canadian ornithologist Leslie Tuck estimates that the world population of this bird (which comes in two species, the thick-billed and the common murre) is not less than 50 million and may run as high as 100 million. He thinks that they are the commonest sea birds in the Northern Hemisphere.

This, despite what seems to be a prodigally careless and wasteful way of life. The murre's single egg is subject to so many hazards that about half the eggs laid never hatch. Many of the casualties roll off the rocks into the sea. Others fall into crevices and cannot be incubated. They get buried in mud and excrement; they roll into puddles. Falling

MURRE EGGS ON THE ROCKS

stones crush them. Plundering gulls get a few more. Some are blown away during high winds. Most of these accidents take place during the first few days of an egg's existence. If something like this happens early enough, the female usually lays again, perhaps in a safer spot. Although they do not build nests, murres have the curious habit of rolling a pebble or two into place next to the egg. This may be a shred of an ancient dream of nest building. It does serve a purpose, for it limits the rolling about of the egg. And as time goes on, the excrement that piles up on the ledge tends to make a kind of glue that binds pebble, egg and rock together. Thus, the longer the egg is on the ledge, the greater its chance of survival. This is further enhanced by the growth of the embryo inside. As it develops, the air sac in the large end gets bigger and bigger, the solid parts within the egg crowd down into the small end, and their weight tends to tip it up more and more, narrowing its rolling radius still farther. A last evolutionary adjustment is that the shell of the small end, the one that comes into abrasive contact with the rock, is measurably thicker than that at the other end.

Murre chicks hatch in a month. They are lively and restless, wandering about the ledge, often soliciting food from adults other than their parents—and sometimes being rewarded. The birds sit close enough to touch each other, and apparently derive great mutual support and security by crowding so tightly. With all this activity on the ledges, and with a constant whirl of clumsy arrivals and departures among the adults, life is as hazardous for the chicks as it was for the eggs. Many fall off the ledges as they explore them, others get knocked or blown off. They fall into cracks and cannot get out. They freeze. They get squashed and suffocated during bad storms when all the adolescent and unmated birds that might normally spend the night on the water come piling up on the nesting sites.

A GUANO-STREAKED LOOMERY: MURRES ABOVE, KITTIWAKES BELOW

Still another hazard that the chick must survive is the temptation to leave the ledge before it is old enough to do so safely. As the chick population reaches the age of about three weeks, waves of increasing excitement run through the colony. There is a tremendous amount of flying back and forth between ledges and the sea. Tension mounts until finally it becomes unbearable. One evening the youngsters will suddenly begin leaping off. They cannot fly. They pump their little wings madly, and the best most of them can achieve is a steep glide that carries them to the water. Others smash themselves on the rocks. Adults swoop down with them, cluster excitedly about those that reach the water, and after a period of milling and diving, one chick and one adult (not necessarily its parent, but one that has adopted it to take it out to sea) will swim off together.

I wish I could observe this mass launching, but the chicks we are looking at now on the ledges at Cape St. Mary's are too small. They will not go for another couple of weeks. They are still covered with baby down, which must be converted to real feathers before they can venture into the water.

One great danger for a downy chick that may be a few days younger than most of the crowd is that it will be caught up in the frenzy of departure and will prematurely hurl itself over the cliff along with the others. Adults sometimes try to prevent this by standing in the way in rows. They are not always success-

ful and the youngster makes the fatal leap. It may even reach the water, but without true feathers it will lack buoyancy. Bedraggled and exhausted, it will paddle about desperately, slowly sinking deeper until it finally drowns. At most of the big loomeries gulls and foxes make a good living scavenging among the rocks below the breeding ledges.

What a contrast there is between the murres and their neighbors, the kittiwakes. The kittiwake is a small and surpassingly graceful gull. It has none of the headlong, unstable, must-keep-flapping-or-I'll-drop style of the murre. It is as light and airy as a feather. With the strong updrafts that blow among these cliffs, the kittiwake seems self-levitating. It dances and balances on nothing, tilting wingtip or tail, edging the cliff face, finally lighting with the utmost delicacy on a tiny ledge not more than three inches wide. All the kittiwakes can do this. And they glue their nests all over the face of the cliff, anchoring them on tiny projections that seem scarcely big enough to support a swallow. What is more,

KITTIWAKE NESTLINGS

A GANNET METROPOLIS ON CAPE ST. MARY'S

gulls? I puzzle about this, watching them as they float effortlessly in front of me, riding a wind that whistles around this cliff, carrying a driving rain upward so that I am as wet under the chin as I am on top of my head. I finally decide it must be the kittiwake's eyes—dark and gentle looking. I see herring gulls as vicious predators because I have watched them carry off little ducklings. And they have heartless yellow eyes. Kittiwakes do not prey on ducklings or on each other's young. They are the most seagoing of all gulls and live by scooping macroplankton from the surface of the open ocean. And their eyes *are* dark and soulful. But that soulfulness depends on one's point of view. To a tiny fish, a kittiwake's eye must have the sudden and terrible blackness of oblivion, the end of everything.

Beyond this rock face is another, and then another, all alive with murres and kittiwakes, each crack lined with them like lice in a wrinkle. Farther down the coast is a domelike headland that seems to be covered with snow.

It is this one that we have come particularly to see, for that snow cap is actually a carpet of nesting birds: gannets. We walk inland to get around some intervening chasms and again approach the coast, finding that we can come out on a pinnacle of rock not 50 yards from the top of this nesting ground.

Here on about a quarter of an acre sit 3,000 stunning birds. Bigger than gulls, they have long scimitar-sharp bills of a pale gray blue edged with

there are plump gray chicks in the nests or standing on the ledges. But the peril of their situation seems to be well understood. Unlike the reckless, strolling murres, each kittiwake nestling is motionless, its bill pointed resolutely at the cliff face as if it might be overcome by vertigo if it

turned around and looked over the edge. The parents, sitting quietly beside them, also face inward; often they are forced to stand almost upright, so narrow is their perch.

What is there about kittiwakes that makes them seem so different from their relatives, the herring

PARENT AND YOUNG SHARING A GANNET NEST

black where it meets the face. Their eyes are a startling white ringed with brilliant turquoise. Their heads are a creamy yellow color, their wingtips black. Otherwise they are pure white. All this we can see through our telephoto lenses as if we were standing over them. They are spaced at intervals, each on a large nest far enough from the next nest so that a bird reaching to peck from one just reaches the bill tip of a bird reaching from another. Thus do gannets deal with the tensions of crowding.

The sitting birds are only half the colony. Another 3,000 are in the air or in the water below. The fliers soar in on stiff wings over the nests, flying fast, but scarcely moving in the 30-mile wind that is tearing over the headland. Squadrons of birds station themselves motionless in front of us, their feathers rippling in the wind. Some are carrying bits of nesting material, but most are just cruising by with heads cocked to observe the nest area below. They are swimming on a tremendous ocean of air. For the first time in my life I get a sense of what it must be like to be a bird and ride these currents.

On and on the squadrons come in a great wheeling circle, sailing slowly over the cliff top, then veering out to sea and disappearing downwind at an incredible speed. I take picture after picture, leaning heavily on my tripod to hold it steady in the wind, cleaning the rain off the lens every couple of minutes. Never have I had a better chance to shoot crowds of big birds close up in flight. I am wildly excited (and will be correspondingly despairing two weeks later when I get back home and find my camera was broken).

A bird suddenly drops on the nesting area to greet its mate. The two stand face to face, their breasts touching, their heads and long bills pointing straight up. They rattle their bills together and say "urragh" in loud guttural tones. There are other "urraghs" coming from all sides, other gestures: lowered heads, quick jabs with bills, tugs of war over nesting material, curtsies with a head tucked under a raised wing. Another bird lands. More sword rattling and a series of urgent "uk-uk-uk-uk-uks" from its chick. The parent lowers its head and the chick greedily thrusts its entire head down the parent's throat to feed on regurgitated fish. Then it withdraws its head, apparently satisfied, for it sits down and closes its eyes. Meanwhile the other parent, displaced from the nest, waddles to one side, aims its bill at the sky, says "yorr" in a loud voice, turns in a tight circle with deliberate stamping feet and leaps into the air. I follow it with my binoculars. Down it planes on wings as rigid as bars. It levels off a hundred feet from the water, hovers there a moment, then suddenly drops into the sea in a nearly vertical dive. A 10-foot plume of spray shoots into the air.

What magnificent birds! Like the common terns of my Massachusetts home, gannets make their living by cruising above the water and diving on fish that they see. But they are the square or the cube of terns, tern-Herculeses who, if they were not so

gracefully streamlined, should surely be bulging with muscles. They exude power and speed. And those dives! Fishermen claim to have recovered gannets caught in nets at depths of 180 feet. Scientists question the possibility of this. But they concede that gannets are good underwater swimmers and can probably get down a hundred feet. They are known to take fish of up to two pounds in size.

Cape St. Mary's is one of three major gannetries along the Northeast coast. Another is on Funk Island, once the home of the great auk, and is virtually inaccessible. Another, at Bonaventure Island off the Gaspé Peninsula, is the best known and the most easily reached. It has more birds than Cape St. Mary's, but the concentration here is denser and the setting grander: an endless procession of gliding birds against elemental cliffs and a stormy sea that, from the viewer's vantage point, seems to stretch 50 miles to the horizon.

What it might be like here on another day with the wind in a different quarter I have no idea. Perhaps the birds cannot fly and hang in the air as they do now. But this day has been one to fill the heart. I have been so saturated with the experience that I notice only now that I have been here seven hours and am staggering under the burden of a heavy camera bag, a big tripod, two sweaters, a quilted parka and a thick oilskin jacket. The rain is now really driving. Visibility is dropping to zero as the sky darkens. I take a last look at the gannets and go.

NO VACANCIES: GANNETS HOVERING ABOVE A CROWDED NESTING GROUND

6/ The Grandeur of Desolation

*In the high barrens, where a plover's cry died of loneliness
and the soil was barely an inch over bedrock, the black
spruce triumphed...prostrate but powerful, insignificant
but long-enduring.*   FRANKLIN RUSSELL/ *SEARCHERS AT THE GULF*

Since the start of transatlantic jet travel, some millions of Americans
have passed over Newfoundland, yet not one in a hundred thousand
has ever stopped there. Do they wonder about it as they scud by? I
don't know. I have flown over it myself a number of times and have always looked down at it with intense curiosity. From a height of five or
six miles the land looks empty and featureless except for the great
arms of the sea that penetrate its coasts. There are also lakes to be seen
—long thin ones. Surrounding them are trackless stretches of forest,
broken at intervals by some kind of barren tundra. Only by looking in-
tently at the coast as it unreels beneath the airplane's wing am I able to
make out any sign of human presence. Gradually my eyes begin to pick
out huddles of houses at the heads of the coves that wrinkle the coast.
It is as if bits of village breathing space had been chewed out of a forest that elsewhere comes as close to the sea as rock and cliff permit.
    What is the interior of this unmarked northern wilderness really like?
For years I had wanted to know. Now, thanks to the chance that brought
me to the bird rookeries of Great Island and Cape St. Mary's, I was
about to get a glimpse of parts of Newfoundland other than offshore islands and cliffs plunging into the sea.
    I came to love Newfoundland. It is not to everybody's taste, I am
sure. It is often cold and foggy. It rains a good deal. But the cold is bracing to me. A summer day here is like a winy autumn day at home. The ar-

omatic smell that pours out of the woods is indescribably sweet and exhilarating. Being able to strike off almost anywhere into those woods along a bumpy logging road and not see a house or another human being for the next 40 or 50 miles excites me.

The forest is primarily spruce and balsam fir. The spruce comes in two kinds: white and black, the latter, mixed with tamarack, mostly found in lower, boggier areas. Walking in the forest is next to impossible; one must find a track and follow that. Even where the land has been lumbered, the young trees that are coming back grow in a stifling thickness. Few birds sing here, and few small plants grow in the barren soil beneath the trees. In the bottom land the ground is covered with a mat of sphagnum moss that holds rain water like a sponge.

I ventured inland one day, into a part of southeastern Newfoundland that has been set aside as a forest and animal preserve in the center of the Avalon Peninsula. There is a large lake back in there with a dam for water power, and I was able to drive for six or eight miles on the dam road before it became impassable and I had to continue on foot. I had been told that a herd of caribou lived in this area, and I was hoping for a glimpse of them. The land rose as I walked. Soon the forest dwindled away and I came out on a rolling upland where nothing grew but low bushes and tufts of grass. Here was primordial undigested soil of a barrenness beyond belief, where the skin of the continent had been scraped off by glacial ice to reveal the rock bone beneath. Splinters of it lay everywhere, boulders sitting on slabs, pebbles on boulders, gravel chips strewn about so haphazardly that they seemed to have been thrown there yesterday—except that they could have been lying just as I found them for 5,000 years, with nothing to disturb them but the wind that was now roaring across this waste and the frost that might next winter crack a pebble or two in half.

Ahead was the lake, torn by whitecaps, curving among some low hills. Whenever I topped a rise I sat down with my binoculars and looked for caribou. I didn't see one. I didn't see anything, in fact, except some fox sparrows and, when I got to the lakeshore, a single greater yellowlegs that went squealing off down the wind.

The scarcity of birds in this part of the country is not surprising. The uplands of Newfoundland are barren, the woods contain only a few kinds of vegetation and seem to be attractive only to kinglets, blackpoll warblers and chickadees. The best places to see birds are where the forest has been cut—along the roads, in logged clearings, on the edges of farm pastures where spruce gives way to alder, birch and to berry bushes. Here fox sparrows and whitethroats abound, singing beautiful haunting songs that I never hear at home. When these birds visit the States in the cold months they are silent. Another bird whose song was unfamiliar to me was the pine grosbeak. Seen in New England only in the dead of winter, in Newfoundland it is one of the commonest song-birds. It is a plump finch the size of a starling, with handsome bricky-pink plumage. It likes to sit in gravel roads, an easygoing bird that will let you walk to within five or six feet of it.

I had a different sort of look at Newfoundland's 42,734 square miles of wilderness near the west coast, where the remnants of a once-mighty mountain range run north for some 120 miles from the lovely inland sea of Bonne Bay. Ages of erosion have ground the mountains down to a tableland scarred by a series of gorges that are dramatically steep, sheer walls of rock. Nowhere are they more breathtaking than around the shores of a lake called Western Brook Pond.

I had been told to keep an eye out for Western Brook Pond as I made my way up the coast. Finally I came to a place that seemed to promise a view of it. For a better look I climbed a gravel bank by the roadside and found myself gazing inland across four or five miles of waving grasses, clumps of bushes and an occasional little steely pond. On the far side of this flat space, distant enough to look blue in the soft north-ern light, rose the walls of a chasm at whose bottom—tantalizingly in-visible from where I stood—lay the lake.

I had to see that lake, and after some inquiry at a nearby village I man-aged to find a guide.

"D'ye own rubber boots?" he asked.

"Boots?"

"It's boggy there, you know."

Boggy it was. What looked like grassland turned out to be a sopping expanse of tundra, a springy bed of sphagnum moss that seemed dry enough until you put a foot on it; then you went down into an inch of water. Narrow muddy trails with enormous animal tracks in them wan-dered through the grass.

"You sure grow big cows around here," I said.

"Them's moose."

I looked into each patch of bushes we passed, hoping—in vain, as it turned out—to glimpse one of those long black Roman moose noses poking out under its umbrella of antlers.

Squish squish, mile after mile. The going seemed easy, but became tiring, like walking in snow. I found myself aiming for little hummocks, any tiny rise that gave promise of a somewhat drier place on which to flop for a moment's rest. The hummocks were springy too, deliciously so. When I spread my arms and legs I found I could loll safely a foot above the water, suspended—as I discovered—on what was actually a miniature forest of dwarf black spruces.

As we walked, the blue chasm that was our goal seemed to grow steadily grayer—and deeper. Finally we pushed through a clump of trees and came out on the water's edge.

Western Brook Pond is absolutely stunning. Imagine a smaller grayer Grand Canyon, set in forest, with a blue lake 10 miles long at its bottom. Or more accurately, a breathlessly steep and narrow fjord—which I am sure this pond was at one time. The unnaturally flat bog we had crossed undoubtedly had been a shelf of coastal sea bottom, and the present pond an arm of that higher sea. Now the pond, fed by the snow that lingers until late July on the tableland far above, is fresh—cold, limpid, rocky bottomed and full of trout.

But the best view, the one I had been promised from the distant road, the one where perpendicular facing cliffs seemed almost to meet, was capriciously hidden behind an intervening outcropping of rock. Was there a way, I asked, of going along the shore to open up the view?

"Too rocky. You'll be needin' a canoe."

"But the view...."

"You made no mention of no view. Said you wanted to see the paand. Here 'tis. Took you the shaartest way."

The guide had. And the shortest way turned out to be too long for me. Going back through the sucking bog, one of my knees gave out. I did the last mile in some pain, stiff-legged.

I never did get the quintessence of Western Brook Pond, but some day I mean to. The next morning I departed. I drove back down the west coast, the blue mountain range on my left, the blue sea on my right, the gray rocks everywhere. Scores of small black horses stood in the fields as I went by, knee-deep in a dazzle of buttercups. What were horses for in a world that made its living from the sea?

"Ain't fer naathin'," said a man I asked. "Them's just pets."

Portrait of a Lonely Island

PHOTOGRAPHS BY JOHN DE VISSER

The portfolio of Newfoundland pictures shown on the following pages is the work of the Canadian photographer John de Visser, who has traveled the length and breadth of his country and favors Newfoundland above all other regions. "Apart from its great people—who have the unique dignity that comes from having to rely on themselves for survival —Newfoundland abounds in special qualities," he says. "Of course it has an enormous variety of gorgeous scenery, which is usually heightened by its closeness to the sea. But that's just the background. Up close, the very big and grand is always being played off against delicate little things in the most dramatic way."

Although he loves the island, de Visser also stands a little in awe of it. "In winter it can be pretty bad. Storms hit that southwest coast with a force that can actually frighten you. And it's easy to get lost in the woods because the fog rolls in from the ocean quickly and unexpectedly. I always carry a compass inland."

But these are the very features that endear Newfoundland to de Visser. "Everywhere I have the feeling that I'm only a step or so away from true wilderness. It is that feeling that excites me as a photographer—that, and the experience of always finding something new or beautiful in the next coastal bay or inland forest clearing. Newfoundland is indeed a paradise for a photographer—if he has warm underwear."

THE LONG RANGE MOUNTAINS BENEATH A RISING MOON

WINTER SEAS POUNDING THE SOUTHWEST COAST

A STONY STRETCH OF THE GREAT NORTHERN PENINSULA

CUMULUS CLOUDS OVER DEER LAKE

A TRACKLESS SPRUCE AND FIR FOREST, TERRA NOVA NATIONAL PARK

"OLD MAN'S BEARD" FESTOONING DEAD BRANCHES

MAJESTIC BREAKERS IN BONAVISTA BAY

THE SPARKLE OF A SMALL RIVER

KELP TWINING AMONG PEBBLES

SUMMER SUNSHINE ON A STERN SHORE

AN INLAND LAKE FROM A HILL OF DAISIES

VIBURNUM FLOWERS EDGING A WATERFALL NEAR THE HUMBER RIVER

MORNING FOG IN BONAVISTA BAY

Bibliography

*Also available in paperback.
†Available in paperback only.

Berrill, N. J. and Jacquelyn, *1001 Questions Answered about the Seashore.* Dodd, Mead & Company, 1959.

Bigelow, Henry B. and William C. Schroeder, *Fishes of the Gulf of Maine,* Fishery Bulletin of the Fish and Wildlife Service, Vol. 53, 1953.

Braun, E. Lucy, *Deciduous Forests of Eastern North America.* The Blakiston Company, 1950.

Buchsbaum, Ralph, *Animals without Backbones.* The University of Chicago Press, 1948.

†Carson, Rachel, *The Edge of the Sea.* Signet Science Library, 1955.

*Hay, John and Peter Farb, *The Atlantic Shore.* Harper and Row, 1966.

King, Judith E., *Seals of the World.* Trustees of the British Museum (Natural History), 1964.

King, Philip B., *The Evolution of North America.* Princeton University Press, 1959.

Kingsbury, John M., *The Rocky Shore.* The Chatham Press, 1970.

Prudden, T. M., *About Lobsters.* The Bond Wheelwright Company, 1970.

Lockley, R. M., *Grey Seal, Common Seal.* October House, 1966.

Lockley, R. M., *Puffins.* The Devin-Adair Company, 1953.

MacGinitie, G. E. and Nettie, *Natural History of Marine Animals.* McGraw-Hill, Inc., 1968.

Matthews, Leonard Harrison, *The Whale.* Simon and Schuster, 1968.

Mowat, Farley and John de Visser, *This Rock within the Sea: A Heritage Lost.* Little, Brown and Company, 1968.

National Film Board of Canada, *Canada: A Year of the Land.* 1967.

Peattie, Donald Culross, *A Natural History of Trees of Eastern and Central North America.* Houghton Mifflin Company, 1950.

Rich, Louise Dickinson, *The Coast of Maine.* Thomas Y. Crowell Company, 1970.

*Russell, Franklin, *Searchers at the Gulf.* W. W. Norton & Company, Inc., 1970.

Russell, Franklin, *The Atlantic Coast.* N.S.L. Natural Science of Canada Limited, 1970.

*Russell, Franklin, *The Secret Islands.* W. W. Norton & Company, 1966.

Scheffer, Victor, *Seals, Sea Lions and Walruses.* Stanford University Press, 1958.

Simpson, Dorothy, *The Maine Islands in Story and Legend.* J. B. Lippincott Company, 1960.

Slipjer, E. J., *Whales.* Basic Books, Inc., 1962.

Tuck,, Leslie M., *The Murres.* Department of Northern Affairs and National Resources, National Parks Branch, Canadian Wildlife Series, 1960.

Acknowledgments

The author and editors of this book wish to thank the following: B. E. Barrett, Department of Natural Sciences, Roger Williams College, Bristol, Rhode Island; Gerard Boardman, South Street Seaport Museum, New York City; Maud Bruemmer, Montreal, Quebec; Canadian Government Travel Bureau, Ottawa, Ontario; John N. Cole, Editor, *Maine Times,* Topsham, Maine; Consulate General of Canada, New York City; Leverett B. and Eugenie Davis, Newcastle, Maine; E. V. Earnshaw, The New Brunswick Museum, Saint John, New Brunswick; Leslie Eastman, Old Orchard Beach, Maine; Paul G. Favour Jr., Northeast Harbor, Maine; C. Bruce Fergusson, Provincial Archivist, Public Archives, Halifax, Nova Scotia; F. Burnham Gill, Provincial Archivist, Provincial Archives, St. John's, Newfoundland; John M. Good, former Superintendent, Acadia National Park; Ann Guilfoyle, Senior Editor, *Audubon,* National Audubon Society, New York City; Sidney Horenstein, Department of Invertebrate Paleontology, The American Museum of Natural History, New York City; Charles E. Huntington, Professor of Biology, Bowdoin College, Brunswick, Maine; Richard Huyda and Beatrice Larose, Public Archives of Canada, Ottawa, Ontario; Gerald T. Iles, Canadian Audubon Society, Montreal, Quebec; Niels W. Jannasch, Curator, Marine History, Nova Scotia Museum, Halifax; Mariette Magnan, Quebec Government House, New York City; A. W. Mansfield, Director, Fisheries Research Board of Canada, Ste. Anne de Bellevue, Quebec; John McKee, Brunswick, Maine; J. C. Medcof, Fisheries Research Board, Atlantic Biological Station, St. Andrews, New Brunswick; Lorraine Monk, National Film Board of Canada, Ottawa, Ontario; Duryea Morton, Director of Educational Services, National Audubon Society, New York City; Dalton Muir, Canadian Wildlife Service, Ottawa, Ontario; The Nature Conservancy, Arlington, Virginia; New Brunswick Travel Bureau, Fredericton; Newfoundland and Labrador Tourist Development Office, St. John's, Newfoundland; Nova Scotia Information Service, Halifax; Christopher M. Packard, Brunswick, Maine; Larry Pardue, The New York Botanical Garden, New York City; Freeman W. Patterson, Toronto, Ontario; Fred H. Phillips, Provincial Archives, Fredericton, New Brunswick; Prince Edward Island Travel Bureau, Charlottetown; Kenneth R. H. Read, Concord, Massachusetts; Keith Ronald, University of Guelph, Ontario; Carl P. Silsby, Maine Department of Economic Development, Augusta; David E. Sergeant, Fisheries Research Board of Canada, Ste. Anne de Bellevue, Quebec; George H. Taylor, State of Maine Department of Sea and Shore Fisheries, Augusta; Stanley G. Triggs, Notman Photographic Archives, McCord Museum, McGill University, Montreal, Quebec; Elinor Voss, Confederation Centre Library, Charlottetown, Prince Edward Island; Shirley E. Welch, Maine Historical Society, Portland.

Picture Credits

The sources for the pictures in this book are shown below. Credits for the pictures from left to right are separated by commas.

Cover—John de Visser. Front end papers 1, 2—Freeman Patterson. Front end paper 3, page 1—John McKee. 2, 3—Dalton Muir. 4, 5—Fred Bruemmer. 6, 7—John de Visser. 8, 9—Charles Pratt. 10, 11—Bullaty Lomeo. 12, 13—Arthur Swoger. 18, 19—Map by R. R. Donnelley Cartographic Services. 31 through 39—John de Visser. 45 through 57—Bullaty Lomeo. 60, 61—Robert Walch. 64, 65—John McKee, William H. Amos. 68, 69, 71—William H. Amos. 73—D. E. Aiken. 76, 77—D. E. Aiken. 78—Douglas Faulkner. 79—Kenneth R. H. Read. 82 through 85—William H. Amos. 101, 102, 103—Notman Photographic Archives, McCord Museum of McGill University. 104, 105—New Brunswick Provincial Archives, The Public Archives of Canada. 106, 107—Courtesy Premier Joseph Smallwood, Newfoundland. 108, 109—Andrew Merrilees Collection. 110, 111—Andrew Merrilees Collection, courtesy Martin R. (Mac) Lee. 112, 113—Maine Historical Society. 127 through 137—Fred Bruemmer. 139—John de Visser. 140 through 143—Maitland A. Edey. 144, 145—Charles E. Huntington. 146—Christa Armstrong from Rapho-Guillumette. 147—Roman Bittman. 149—Fred Bruemmer. 150 through 153—Dan Guravich. 154—John de Visser. 155—Will Lamoreux. 156, 157—John de Visser. 163 through 179—John de Visser.

Index

Printed in U.S.A. **X**